MURDER
AT THE
CORNERS

MURDER
AT THE
CORNERS

by G. B. RAY

NorTex
Press

Reprint of the original 1957 edition.

Additional copies are available from the
Whitewright Public Library,
PO Box 984, Whitewright TX 75491
(903) 364-2955

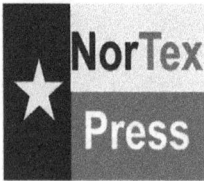

Introduction

THIS BOOK WILL RELATE THE ACTIVITIES OF people classified as desperadoes, scalawags, guerrillas, Jay-Hawkers, and Red Legs, who resided, some permanently, some temporarily, in the vicinity of Pilot Grove, Hog Eye, Choctaw Bottom, Wildcat Thicket and Jernigan Thicket, all in North Texas, in the days of Reconstruction — 1865-1870.

A desperado, as used in this book, was very often a Confederate veteran who found himself through force of circumstances outlawed by local society and labeled a renegade by the "New Order." He was also many times a gentleman with nothing but worthless Confederate money in his pockets. Every local crime was charged to his credit; sometimes legally so; many times, illegally.

A scalawag was usually a Union sympathizer who had "laid in the brush" during the four-year war to escape conscription by the Southern army, or else he was a Confederate deserter, or else again he was a Northern man hiding from conscription by the Northern army.

The Jay-Hawkers were the wandering refugees or veterans from Kansas and Missouri, looking for a new life and new land on the frontier, or they were running away from a disgraceful past.

The Red Legs were Kansans with about the same ideas as the Missourians, except the Red Legs were an official organization of Union sympathizers and Home Guards formed to protect Kansas from invasion by Confederates. Both groups waged guerrilla and border warfare and some became enamored of it.

THE CORNERS — was the area where the boundaries of the four counties touched. The oldest settlement and headquarters of the area was at Pilot Grove, often called Lickskillet, because of the poverty and hunger experienced by the people there during the years of the War, 1861-1865.

The counties of Grayson, Fannin, Collin, and Hunt were fairly well-settled and prosperous when the war began; yet it must be kept in mind that, in comparison with the settlements of Central Texas, this country north of the Brazos was new country. Two of these four counties — Grayson and Fannin — touched Red River on the north, and just beyond that was the Indian Nation — a strange unknown land full of red men.

The village of Pilot Grove had one of the earliest post offices in the region and was on the main stage line running from Jefferson and Clarksville south to Waco. The village, often called the "Corners", the "Skillet" and the "Grove", was perched just over the Grayson County line, but it was only a couple of miles to the Fannin County line, the Collin County line, or the Hunt County line. It was also about equi-distant from the capitals of these counties: namely, about twenty-five miles from Sherman, Bonham, McKinney, or Greenville. In the story we are about to relate, the characters and the action will move from one to the other of these four towns. Twenty-five miles was a mighty trip in those days of cowpaths and horse trails, bridgeless creeks, and heavy thickets.

Other and smaller communities lay along this route; there was Dog Town, a community very near the Skillet and just west of the present community of Desert; Hog-Eye, a popular spot, was just over the Hunt County line and near the present town of Celeste.

WILD-CAT THICKET: The strip of land in Fannin and Hunt lying just east of the Corners was a solid mass of undergrowth — trees, briar bushes, thorn vines and grass. It was so thick and heavy that it was almost impossible to get through it or see through it, even in daytime. Hence, it became the perfect hiding place for army deserters and slackers of both North and South; refugees from the North seeking to evade military service; robbers and criminals of all sorts. It became the *locus operandi* in the feud between the Lee and Peacock parties in the days of Reconstruction.

Jenigan Thicket, Black Jack Grove, Choctaw Bottom — these were also prominent spots of rendezvous and hideaway. They were similar to Wildcat, except that perhaps they were not as secure in their fastnesses, but in any one of them a man could feel pretty safe from soldiers, sheriffs, posses, friends or foes.

When the war began, many young men of the CORNERS went away to fight for the Confederacy and some did not return until the War had ended. While they were gone, their home community underwent a change; people from Kansas, Missouri, Iowa, Kentucky, Arkansas and other states moved in. A pro-Union feeling developed. Grayson County was strongly in favor of the Union and voted against secession at the election held in 1862. The Corners became a popular spot for newcomers, whether well-to-do settlers or runaway draft dodgers.

GUERRILLAS — were the wandering soldiers from Missouri who preyed upon the community when necessary, or joined its respectable citizenry when they desired. Quantrell and his men, and Anderson and his men liked the Corners; they visited it frequently. Grayson, Fannin and Cooke being border counties, the Missouri guerrillas found them convenient hiding spots on the route from Missouri, the Indian Territory and across the Red; besides that, the citizens of these counties liked the guerrillas, generally speaking. Some stayed to become respectable, permanent citizens of Texas. Their antipathy was for Union sympathizers, Union soldiers, Union Leaguers, and freedmen who followed the Union League's instructions.

BUSHWHACKER — a trifling sort of fellow who hid out in the brush most of the time to avoid army service and other responsibilities; he got his living by preying on his fellow citizens in any manner that was easy for him. Sometimes he was a Southerner, and oftentimes a Northerner running away from a shady past.

Acknowledgments

MANY PEOPLE HAVE HELPED ME WRITE THIS book. During a period of ten years I have talked with men and women who held vivid memories of the Lee-Peacock War, either from their childhood experiences or from the true accounts passed on to them by their elders.

This period of bloody fighting and tense feeling in the days of Reconstruction — 1865-1870 — is little known outside the section where the fighting took place. The gallant courage and high patriotism displayed by members of both parties will serve to remind us of today that tribulation and war bring hardships and misunderstandings that only peace can cure.

I am particularly idebted to the following people who supplied me with clues, photographs, letters, newspapers and books relating to the characters of this book:

Mr. and Mrs. Bruce Dixon, Route 1, Whitewright, Texas
Mrs. Ed Ikonen,   E. Walker Street, Denison, Texas
Mr. R. E. Gentry   Whitewright, Texas
Mr. H. M. Gentry   Whitewright, Texas

* Mrs. Fannie Gentry Golden   Blue Ridge, Texas
  Mrs. A. R. McMurry   Whitewright, Texas
  Mr. Mal Jackson   Route 1, Whitewright, Texas
* Mr. W. N. Stone   Whitewright, Texas
* Jim Tate   Route 1, Whitewright, Texas
  Mr. Herbert Smith   Dallas, Texas
  Mr. Edgar Smith   Dallas, Texas
  Mr. Lon Bradley   Leonard, Texas
  Mrs. Gyp Sloan   Route 1, Whitewright, Texas
  Miss Mary Connelly   Route 2, Whitewright, Texas
  Mr. Gus Holmes   Trenton, Texas
* Mr. Ed McMahon   Dallas, Texas
* Mr. G. N. White   Blue Ridge, Texas
* Mrs. M. A. Mangrum   Whitewright, Texas
  Mrs. Elizabeth Penn Enos, E. Federal St., Shawnee, Texas
  Mrs. Lillian R. Coffey, 1405 W. 11th St., Plainview, Texas
* Miss Harriet Smithers, State Archivist,
    State Archives   Austin, Texas
  Mrs. Robert Brandt, Ass't. State Archivist,
    Texas State Library   Austin, Texas
  Mrs. Marcelle Lively Hamer, City Library, El Paso, Texas
  Mr. Wm. Shirriff, State Land Office   Austin, Texas
  Mrs. Adah Truett Gillespie   Whitewright, Texas

Whitewright and Austin, Texas
January, 1957   G. B. RAY

---

* Deceased

Prologue – Voice of the Corners:

Early Spring — 1955

Dear Reader:

We had another murder at the Corners last week. Ain't nothing unusual about that; such things has been happening in this neck of the woods for more'n eighty years. The way it's done sometimes changes, such as this fellow last week. He was found dead — burnt to a cinder — all tucked into his bed as neat as a pin — not even a sign of a scorch on the bedclothes. Well, a little corner of the wallpaper was scorched, and there was a bucket with some water in it that looked sorter like there'd been some papers burned in it. Course they -- I mean the sheriff and his men — found some blood stains on the floor, and the man's blue jeans was out in the yard a piece, but as to who done it, or why, they ain't found out nothing yet. If it was done for spite or grudge that ain't no way to do a murder of that sort. It's fairer, and it's more exciting, too, to meet and shoot it out like they done in the days of Bob Lee and Bill Penn. Then a fellow could carry as many guns as he could afford to buy; them was the days of six-shooters and shotguns, and they wore them in their belts, under their vests, and over their shoulders and saddle-horns, when they took to the road. We had a heap of killings around here then; ain't never been a time like it. It's to be hoped there never will be again. When there's between fifty and one hundred men killed and it's strung out for five or six years — why — that ain't no makeshift, little stuff; that's blood and thunder, and that's what we had here at The Corners. It all started in 1865 — when Bob Lee come home from war — . . .

Contents

Capt. Robert J. Lee

Dick Johnson

"Parson" Martin W. Gentry

-- Courtesy R. E. Gentry

W. N. Stone and "Uncle" Jim Tate
1952

William Perry (Bill) Penn

Fannie Gentry Golden (1890)
— Courtesy H. M. Gentry

Mrs. Elizabeth H. Penn-Lindsey
— Courtesy Mrs. Elizabeth Penn Enos

Mrs. Letha Penn Beven
-- Courtesy Mrs. Elizabeth Penn Enos

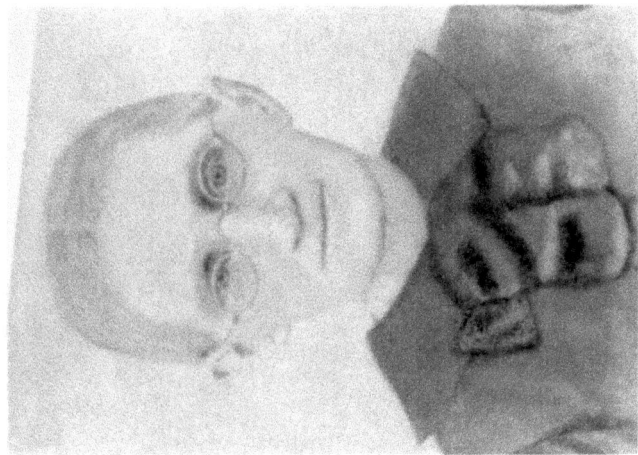

Mrs. Sarah A. Johnson-Dixon
—Courtesy Bruce Dixon

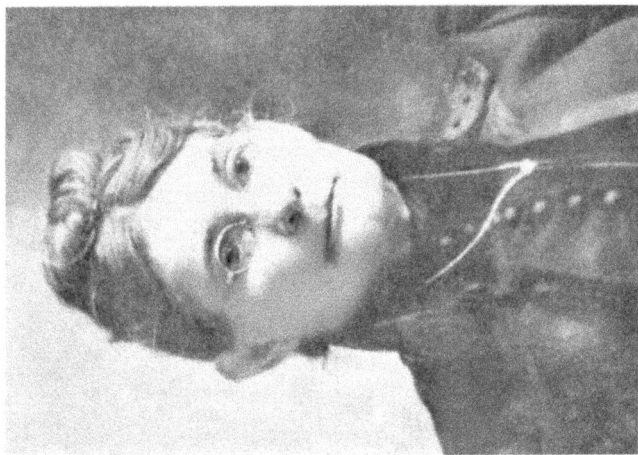

Mrs. Dorinda P. Hancock (1908)
— Courtesy Mrs. Ed. Ikonen

Monument to Capt. Bob Lee
in the old Lee Cemetery, near Leonard, Fannin County

CHAPTER 1

1865

Bob Lee Comes Home

WHEN CAPTAIN ROBERT J. LEE TURNED HIS WAR horse toward Texas in the spring of 1865 he expected to find peace along the way, and at the Corners, that garden spot in the northeast section of the state he called home. It was not within the remotest fringes of his dreams that he would become the heart and core of a vendetta that for sheer hatred would exceed the bitterness that had kept the North and South at war for four years. When he rode west from Memphis, with his destination Lee Station in Fannin County, his thoughts were happy ones about a new era of peace. He did not believe it could be possible for the next four years to be worse than the four years just ended. He lived exactly four more years to disprove his dream.

His war record with the Confederate armies was one of which he was justly proud. He had left home as a Private in the Texas State Troops; he was returning a Captain of Cavalry with the Army of Tennessee. He had a good horse and side-arms, and it was pleasing to know that he had not had to surrender either.

Many hours of his trip homeward he spent recalling his wife Melinda and their three children. "O, My sweet Melinda Lee!" He hummed a tune to fit his thoughts.

On a hot August afternoon in 1861 he had ridden over to Pilot Grove to enlist. There he had signed up with a company of volunteers for the Texas State Troops under Captain Jackson E. McCoole. That patriotic and impulsive act altered the course of his life and launched him upon a career that was to be short and dangerous. It marked the end of his life as a private citizen, living in contentment with his small family on the Lee land in Fannin and Hunt Counties. It had been seven years since he had married Melinda Mahan — December 4, 1854, the records in Bonham show — and brought his sweet Melinda to live at Lee's Station.

The Governor had issued a call for three thousand troops to help the Confederacy. Bob and Melinda agreed that when a man had to go fight a war, the sooner he started the sooner he'd get it finished and come back to his own affairs. If Texas was in trouble it was a man's duty to help out. So he rode to Lickskillet, blissfully unaware that his years of happiness had been terminated by Texas' secession and a fast-gathering war. Although Texas was a mighty long way from the scene of battle, the war feeling had already enveloped the state. Companies of volunteers to serve as Home Guards only, within the borders of the state, sprang up all along the 700 miles from the Red River to the Rio Grande. Strong young men who believed it would be a short war went rapidly to the settlements to enlist in a war destined to be long and cruel.

Such was the case at Pilot Grove. Captain McCoole had come there to raise a company because the Corners was a popular meeting place. There were good farms and good farmers in that area of Grayson, Fannin, Hunt, and Collin. Therefore, Colonel W. B. Sims of Sherman, who set out to raise a regiment, sent Captain McCoole to Pilot Grove to raise at least one company.

It was the end of August, the 29th, hot and dry, and time to pick cotton, but the Captain got his company. Bob Lee was one of them. He gave his age as 27. Captain McCoole didn't tarry about his business. He took his recruits that very day to Sherman and presented them to Colonel Sims, each man providing his own arms, clothing, — and horse, of course. With a speed and efficiency undreamed by the recruits, they were mustered into the State Troops for a period of twelve months and sent into training quarters at Camp Reeves, Grayson County. But in one month and sixteen days, namely, on October 14, 1861, Colonel Sims' men were considered fit for duty with the C.S.A. and accordingly they were mustered into Confederate service and sent immediately to Arkansas as Company C of the Ninth Texas Cavalry, to serve under Gen. Ben McCulloch. Lee's pay from the state had amounted to $18.40 at the salary of twelve dollars per month. He had been allowed another $18.40 for his horse and $6.38 for clothing issued to him. Thus equipped and trained, Company C had set out on dangerous service.

His ability to ride and shoot served Lee well; by the end of November he had been promoted to Second Lieutenant. That first spell of duty with Company C seemed far away now; they had ridden 450 miles to the place of rendezvous with General McCulloch in Missouri, securing their provisions along the road as best they could. He recalled their camps in the Cherokee Nation, in Arkansas, and back again in East Texas. At Daingerfield he had enlisted with Captain

3

E. R. Hawkins' Texas Fencibles, and not long afterward was transferred to Whitfield's Battery. A year later he was in Mississippi with the same outfit — Whitfield's Legion, sometimes called Whitfield's Battery, a unit that made a distinguished record in the bloody annals of Confederate military history.

Lee re-enlisted for the war, and as time went on he became a Captain, and his commander, Major Whitfield, made Brigadier. The Legion was attached to the Army of Tennessee. The Captain, even now, after the Great Defeat, thrilled with pride when he thought about the many generals he had come to know through battle: Generals Ben McCulloch, Albert Pike, Earl Van Dorn, Henry Forney, Henry Little, N. B. Forrest, and, of course and always, J. W. Whitfield.

The life of a cavalryman had led him far, through hardships, privation, starvation and blood. The Ninth Texas Cavalry had fought at Pea Ridge, Wilson's Creek and Elkhorn Tavern, then across the Mississippi at Corinth, Iuka, Vicksburg, Nashville, Murphreesboro, Missionary Ridge, and the siege of Atlanta. Of their gallant fighting General Ross had said in his reports: "The gallant bearing of the Ninth Texas — is deserving of special commendation — the charges made by them have never been and cannot be surpassed by cavalry of any nation."

He had done most of his fighting east of the Mississippi, but he was well aware of the troublous times now settling on the country west of the Mississippi, particularly on Texas. He was thoroughly familiar with the failure of General Banks' scheme to invade Texas, due to the stout defense of the Army of the Trans-Mississippi.

Now that the war was ended and men were making their way back home, he wondered what he would find at the Corners. Would he find peace or would there be more trouble? If he could believe Melinda's letters, there was little indication of peace at home. Partisan feeling was growing worse instead of better; the Union League was raising its head like a giant in the land. The name TEXAS was anathema in Washington. Because she had not surrendered and would not surrender, steps were to be taken to bring the recalcitrant state into line. Federal troops were to be sent to Texas, whispered Melinda in her letters. Captain Robert Lee, her husband, laughed at the thought. "The Feds in Texas? Oh no, that can never be."

For a man who had lived in the saddle and slept in the open for nearly four years, the five-hundred-mile-ride from Memphis was no chore. The road was marked by returning Confederates: gay, dejected, crippled, strong, foot soldiers and cavalrymen — all were making their ways to their homes in Missouri, Arkansas, Louisiana and Texas. Bob Lee considered himself a lucky devil because he had a better horse to ride than some he passed; he knew too, that he had better clothes than many a man going to Texas. For that he could thank his wife Melinda, and his father and family at home who had used sagaciously the gold pieces that Daniel Lee had brought from Virginia and Missouri in the 1830's and these had tided the family over the war period in slightly better circumstances than some. Bob and his brothers in the Confederate service had not suffered for want of clothing and good boots. Bob wondered if there still could be some of the gold left. All his life his father had told him about the pot of gold they had brought in the wagon train. Bob and his brothers had seen it many times. The gold and its hiding place were as ordinary to them as the furniture in the house on the Lee plantation, but when the war came there was a change of policy. Daniel Lee found a new and safer hiding place for the family treasure.

The day he crossed Red River at Fulton, Arkansas, was a happy one for Captain Lee, and that feeling was magnified to its greatest point three days later when he drew near the vicinity of the Corners. The familiar path that led to Lee's Ranch and home lay before him. When he reached it, with trembling hand he took out his six-shooter, raised it high and fired three shots, the signal he had written to Melinda, then he slid from his horse, and with more vigor than he had ever given the Rebel yell, he yelled "MELINDA!"

Quick as a flash of lightning came the answer: "Bob's home!" Doors opened, children ran, a woman screamed. "Bob's home!" In twenty-four hours every home in the Corners had heard it; the echo of it penetrated the thickets where skulkers, one-time deserters, and future guerrillas lay in hiding. Everywhere the call came: "BOB LEE'S HOME!"

After the first blissful days he rode over to the Skillet to look around. From the first he sensed it was not the same; he was royally welcomed by some, but others looked askance at him and made remarks about him, insinuating that a Captain under Forrest might not be so popular at the Corners. Union sympathizers thereabouts did not admire the set of the Captain's plumed hat, and they both envied and resented the gold coins he carried in the pockets of his good coat. They knew the skill of the six-shooters he wore in his belt, and they dared not speak too loud.

But the whispered word carried far and it wasn't long until the news of Bob Lee's return was known everywhere in the Red River Valley. The Confederate veterans were happy about it for now they felt they had a leader; the freedmen were uneasy and shaking with fear behind their bold bravado; the bushwhackers and scalawags hiding in the thickets so long dared not come out now for fear that Lee and his friends might yet hale them into a court of justice.

The Union sympathizers centered in the Union League resolved to do something about it. Captain Lee, the cavalryman, with his good clothes, his plumed hat and his gold coins, was too big for the Corners, and would have to go. Lewis Peacock at the head of the Union League was firm in his intention of speeding Lee's departure by fair means or foul.

These rumors came back to Bob and Melinda at Lee Station; at first they ignored them, refusing to believe that there was anything less than security and happiness at the Corners, but as the months slipped by and they persisted, Bob recognized them as omens of trouble.

His premonitions were realized when a posse surrounded his house one night, and men dressed in the uniforms of United States soldiers entered the house and announced to the captain that he was under arrest and their orders were to take him to Sherman, the county seat of Grayson, where he would be tried for crimes he had committed during the War. Bob was sick in bed at the time but the possemen would grant no stay and he was forced to dress and ride with them. He recognized Lewis Peacock, Jim Maddox, and one of the Borens. At a point a few miles from the Corners the posse was enlarged by another group of citizens. One of these was recognized as Doc Wilson, a questionable character of the community. Doc rode next to Bob and soon began a conversation bearing on the theme that there was a way out of the situation that would make it easy for everybody. Lee had only to hand out some of his gold and the posse would disappear and Lee would escape any punishment at Sherman. The captain of Forrest's Cavalry refused to listen to him, and the entire posse turned off the main road and struck camp in Choctaw Bottom. Bob pleaded to go to Sherman but his captors ignored him and placed a guard over him and settled down to a waiting game. After thirty-six hours the sick man yielded. He signed a note to Doc Wilson for two thousand dollars, with his father's name as security. Besides that, Lee gave them the twenty-dollar gold coin he had in his pocket and promised them his mule and bridle.

When this "treaty" had been duly signed on paper, the guard was withdrawn and Bob and his brother, who had come along too, were allowed to ride away unharmed.

Perhaps it might have ended there if Bob and his brother had chosen to abide by the terms of the treaty made under duress, but now the ire of the captain was aroused. A sense of injustice weighed heavily on him. He determined to ride to Bonham, the county seat of Fannin, and bring suit in the civil courts against the leaders of the posse. Also, he, his brothers, and his father began to count men who would stand by them — relatives and friends; from these they could form an organization in opposition to the Union League of Peacock and his followers. By these two acts the wheels were set in motion for the deadly feud that soon followed.

Bob did go to Bonham, where he filed charges against the leaders of the posse that had kidnapped him. But the Union Leaguers were too well organized to allow a civil suit to go on; they formed a posse and stormed the little Fannin County jail one night and released their men. Bob evened it up by refusing to pay the note he had signed in Choctaw Bottom. And now the feud was off to a good start. Bob Lee's homecoming in 1865 took on a somber tone and the future years of contemplated peace receded into the dim distance of the unattainable.

CHAPTER 2

1866

Turmoil Begins

CAPTAIN BOB LEE WAS A PERSON WHO MADE staunch friends and stalwart enemies. After his efforts to press a civil suit against his kidnappers had failed, he realized that in the northeast section of Texas the war was not yet over; it was still, as one person told him, "in people's hearts." He, like all Confederate veterans and Southern sympathizers, must be subservient to Northern sympathizers and military rule for some time to come. The decisions of the civil courts were supervised by the Military; justice was administered by a judge who traveled with a military escort. Bob Lee did what many others had already done — he built a hide-out in the brush.

MURDER AT THE CORNERS

A part of Wildcat Thicket was on Lee land and there Bob built his shelter. It was made of black oilcloth boiled in linseed oil to make it water repellent and also indistinguishable. Lee's service with Forrest and Whitfield had taught him the artifices of ambush and camouflage. His hide-out became the meeting place of all his followers and friends and its location was never discovered by his enemies. Captain Bob was the recognized leader of a clan, and if any member got into trouble with the Military, he fled to the hide-out for protection and advice. The Captain never failed to give both.

Among those who knew every turning of that hidden path through the Thicket were the Dixons, friends and neighbors living about five or six miles northwest of Lee land. Jack Dixon was a "full-blooded Irishman" according to his own description, who had emigrated with his family from Missouri to Texas in 1858. Before that the Dixon family had lived in Indiana and Illinois, but after landing in Texas Jack Dixon moved no more; in the region of the Corners he found his home.

While he was still living near Springfield, Jack's wife died, leaving a small son named Simpson. This was the same son who, after seeing service with the Confederate armies, was now a follower of Bob Lee; Simp Dixon was known everywhere in North Texas as a close friend of Lee.

But it was Jack's second wife who shared with him the adventures and dangers of life in Texas. She was a young widow named Sarah Anne Johnson when Jack married her. She too had a small son, Dick Johnson. This little boy who left Missouri in the wagon train for Texas was destined to be remembered in the Red River Valley as the avenger of Bob Lee's death, thereby bringing an end to the Great Feud.

Two other Dixon families came to Texas at the same time — the late 1850's. The men were cousins, and all settled in the fertile river valley of North Texas; one at Blue Ridge in the northern tip of Collin County and less than ten miles from the Corners. He was known as "General" Dixon, though where or how he acquired that title, nobody could say. The other Dixon cousin went on to Black Jack Grove in Hopkins County to make his home. He was called *Doctor* Dixon, though whether that meant he was a practitioner of medicine from a medical school or office, nobody seemed to know or care.

But Jack Dixon bought his one hundred and sixty acres from John Sloan at the Corners, and there he and Sarah Anne set up their new home. He hauled the lumber from Jefferson to build his house and he built it well. Standing atop a little rise of the level land, Dixon's Mound became a landmark; it was close to the main road north and south and handy to the village of Pilot Grove. The house and its inhabitants were bound to become involved in everything that happened at the Corners.

Jack's overland freight business, which he had established soon after his arrival in Texas, had prospered. He accumulated more mules and more wagons. He was an experienced freighter and knew how to handle his shipping. During the war years there had been a greater demand than before for freighting. Huge supplies were sent to Jefferson and shipped from there to Confederate forces. Equally needed were food and merchandise that the Dixon Line brought back to settlers along the route and at the Corners. All that prosperity had vanished the year before with the ending of the war. Times were hard and getting harder; Confederate money was worthless and gold was hard to find. Billy Dixon was fourteen and already a good wagoner, and Charlie, son of the Doctor, had come over from Black Jack and joined his cousin's business. These two boys traveled the road to Jefferson many times.

11

Simp Dixon had come back from service with the Confederates and was trying to help out with the family's business, but he was restless and felt out-of-touch with merchandising and freighting. A lot of local boys who had been gone three and four years felt the same restlessness. They could not find their old way of life. Discontent and poverty had replaced contentment and prosperity while they were away in the swamps and marshes. Hatred and suspicion had crept into the thinking and the conversation of the people they met wherever they went. Union men and refugees would not accept Confederate veterans on any level, and Southern men and women could not stomach the Union Leaguers and their followers.

Simp Dixon and all the family at Dixon's Mound were outspokenly Southern in their sentiments. Besides Charlie and Billy, there were the four girls fast approaching their teens — Hester Anne, Susan, Lydia and Sallie; next were the two small boys — Ennis, who could do a mighty good Rebel yell, and the baby of the family who qualified with his name — Robert Lee. Whether he was named for General Robert Lee of Virginia or for Captain Robert Lee, their neighbor, was sometimes discussed in idle conversation, but the consensus of opinion was that the General did not count for as much as their neighbor did in this section of Texas.

Dick Johnson was at the Mound too, but like his step-brother, Simp, he was restless and dissatisfied with home conditions as he found them. He was talking about riding out West to a new country, but in the meantime he was helping wherever needed at home, with the wagon trains, or at the Hide-out, or on the trails at night.

Bill Penn was another young man who wished for something better. His home was six miles to the north of Dixon's Mound at Kentucky-town. He was only nineteen, but he had seen service with the Home Guards during the war.

12

He got acquainted with the Dixon boys at Jefferson, for Penn too was a freighter. In a small way he operated a freight line from his community to the city on Cypress Bayou by way of Bonham. At Jefferson a fellow met all sorts — veterans, deserters, carpetbaggers, politicians, thugs, and bandits. The young teamster listened to their talk, which was mostly concerned with money — how and where it could be gotten. Bill realized from his own experience that nothing mattered now but gold pieces; all the Confederate paper money that he, his mother and sisters had hidden in boxes at their home in Kentucky-town was valueless since Lee surrendered at Appomattox. He was familiar with the exploits of Captain Bob Lee and his mistreatment by the Military and Union Leaguers after his return home. Penn naturally threw in his sympathies with the Southern party, being intensely Southern in his sentiments; his family were Kentuckians and his father had served with the Confederate armies. He became convinced that Bob Lee's way was the only way in which Southerners could regain the peace and happiness lost in the war.

William Perry Penn was the third child in a family of eight children born to Sanford R. Penn and his wife, Elizabeth Hardin Penn. The family coming from Kentucky in the 1850's had settled at the fast-growing village of Kentucky-town. By the time Bill was a teen-ager, he was expert in the use of the six-shooter and rifle, and well able to take care of himself in any situation. He was a handsome young fellow and looked older than his years. When Sanford Penn died in 1862 while in Confederate service, Bill undertook the support of his mother, sisters, and younger brothers. That was how he got started in the overland freight business. The coming of the Military to Texas had stirred him to a hot fever of resentment. He had no tolerance for the New Order.

13

He would take no back talk from the freedmen and was quick to get into a fist fight with any of them or their white sympathizers. On his return from one of his trips to Jefferson a few months back, he had got into a fight with a freedman, Henry Scales. For this he was reported to the Military and soon afterward arrested for assault and battery. A friend sold his horse to put up the bond for Bill's release; but on the day set for his trial in Sherman, Bill was missing.

The weather had played him a nasty trick; his wagons had bogged down in the black mud and boggy creeks and he had been unable to report to the judge on time. But his intentions were honorable, for he kept his appointment, although a little late. When he reported to the judge at the Courthouse he was greeted with the information that his bond was now forfeited and would have to be paid. This was more than Bill could understand, and he had asked: "Are you sure that's right, Judge?" When the judge answered with a strong affirmative, Bill had picked up his hat and pistols from the nearby table and said: "Then it's good-day to you, Judge," and walked out of the Courthouse and away from the handlers of justice.

From that day on Bill had been counted a fugitive from the law. He got into more and more fights with Union men and freedmen and more skirmishes with the Military. He was openly accused by them of taking part in several robberies, and consequently became more bitter in his denunciation of the Union League and its leaders, and the Military and its methods. He swore that he would never again submit to arrest by them and he rode to Lee's Headquarters in Wildcat Thicket and offered his services to that leader, whenever and wherever needed. His offer meant something, for he was an expert in his use of firearms and in his knowledge of the trails and roads of North Texas. Bill rode away looking for trouble and itching for a fight.

Dr. W. H. Pierce, chief doctor at Pilot Grove, was acquainted with Bill and with the circumstances of his unjust trial. On the several occasions he had seen Bill since that time he had tried to calm the young man's bitter resentment and growing hatred of the Yankees. The doctor realized that Bill could be a dangerous enemy.

Dr. Pierce was an educated, cultured man, who did not wish to become involved in any bloody fist fights, pistol fights, or party discords. Right now his future had a rosy tint to it and happiness dwelt very near him. He had a wife and two young childen, a home, and all the patients he could take care of; his chief desires were to relieve suffering, aid the sick, and do his duty fearlessly.

The Pierce family had come to Texas some ten years ago from Sumner County, Tennessee, and settled first at Cannon, five miles west of Pilot Grove. The father, Benjamin Pierce, was a veteran of the War of 1812, wherein he had served as Special Courier to General Jackson. He had moved into the village of Pilot Grove during the recent War Between the States.

Dorinda Anne, his eighteen-year-old daughter, possessed an outstanding personality. Like her brother the Doctor, she was one of the shining lights of the Pierce family. Dorinda had the fearlessness of the pioneers, coupled with an ambition of driving force. She wanted to get an education and she was a constant reader of books of all kinds that she could beg or borrow from friends and neighbors. She had already completed a course of study at the Seminary in Cannon and was now ready to try teaching. She was just as alert and active physically, for she could ride a horse and shoot a gun as well as any of her brothers, even better than some of them. She was well-informed on the political differences and the increasingly hard feelings developing around her; she was afraid of nobody, and consequently, talked and mingled with the people of both factions. But her real sympathies were with the Lee party and the Southern veterans trying so desperately to adjust themselves to a new way of life. She thoroughly believed that education was the best way to do it.

She had a strong advocate of that same theory in Martin Gentry, a Baptist minister and farmer known far and wide as "Parson" Gentry. He had two sons who had returned from service with the Confederates and he saw that they were like others of their comrades — restless, dissatisfied, and unable to decide on their future. The parson believed that a practical application of Bible principles and as much schooling as it was possible to get, would do much toward solving the veterans' problems. He was well aware of the bitter feelings developing among his neighbors, and of the fears and hatreds between the two factions, but he refused steadfastly to be intimidated by the situation.

The parson and his family had come to Texas in 1844 and settled on a tract of land on Desert Creek. His one hundred and sixty acres of wilderness was a public domain. In the twenty years since then he had cleared the land, planted his crops, gathered his harvests, or stored them for the future. He had not become wealthy, but there was always enough to support his large family. That was all he wanted, for first and last his chief concern was in the establishment of churches. He had ridden the back trails of Fannin, Grayson, Collin and Hunt until his name was a household word in the Red River Valley.

When the war ended in '65 the parson was left a widower with thirteen children. When John and William returned from the war, Ma was not there to welcome them; in her stead there was the newest baby, little blue-eyed Fannie. The parson accepted his lot and surmounted his difficulties with good grace. He held his family together. His older girls were in their teens and they could help the younger ones with their tasks.

The parson heard reports of men being shot from ambush; of Federal men in blue scouring the woods for Lee's men; of Union Leaguers inciting the freedmen to action. He knew that his boys had been more than once to the Hide-out in Wildcat Thicket. He took no recognition of that fact or of the many rumors going around. He continued to hold family prayers, to read the Scriptures to his family, and to plow and plant his crops. It was like this when he brought home his second wife, Elizabeth. . . . . . She was a young widow with three children. These three, added to the parson's group, made sixteen children, grown, half-grown, and young fry.

In the midst of shootings, killings and fearful rumors, there were still parties and beaux for the girls to talk about; Mary Anne was being squired by Dow Nance and there seemed to be an "understanding" between them, as she explained to her sisters and younger brothers. The Nance farm was in the same neighborhood, and it seemed that Dow was inclined to follow Peacock and his Union Leaguers. Mary Anne ignored his politics and blissfully planned her wedding as the turmoil increased in violence.

One of the places visited regularly by the parson was Porter's Church in Fannin County. A few months back an incident had occurred there that the parson could not forget, although he carefully avoided telling it at home. A ten-year-old boy named Bill Stone often came to hear him preach. The parson noted the boy that Sunday walking around the churchyard before services. The boy wore a cap with a feather in it, but the parson paid little attention to it at the time.

As a matter of fact, the boy did not pay much attention to the preacher either. When sermon time came he went in and tried to listen to him but his mind wandered repeatedly to the stories he had heard about the parson and his sixteen children; about the Lees and the Peacocks and what the grownups called The Trouble at Pilot Grove. He had been thinking about it that morning when he started to church and that was why he had stuck a peacock feather in his cap. Things were pretty dull and he just wondered if anybody would notice his feather. Sure enough, somebody did.

It happened after church while the women were setting the table for dinner in the yard. Bill and several of his companions were crowding in and sniffing and sampling whenever they could, when suddenly a young man on horseback rode up to the churchyard entrance and surveyed the scene. He did not dismount and one of the boys whispered to Bill: "Hey, that's Simp Dixon; you better watch out." The young man on horseback must have heard it too, for he turned in and rode by them, snatched the feather from Bill's cap with the comment: "Take that damned thing off! We don't like peacocks around here." With that he rode away as quickly as he had come, but all day Bill had something interesting to remember. So did the parson, but for a different reason. He thought it was an omen of danger.

Bill didn't know it then, but there was a ten-year-old Negro boy called Jim Tate, living at the Dave Tate farm between Desert Creek and Pilot Grove, who was destined to become a loyal friend and customer of Stone's in later years. Jim was born in Tennessee in slavery days and had come with his young master, Dave Tate and family to the Corners region in the 1850's. Jim said he remembered hearing something the year before about 'Mancipation but he didn't pay "no 'tention" to it; he just stayed on the farm and minded Mr. Dave. His "white folks" were good to him and Jim was as happy as the long summer days of Texas. Sometimes he went to "Mr. Peacock's place" and played with John and Cathy; sometimes to the parson's, where he played with the Gentry boys, and many times to Mr. Jack Dixon's, where he helped Mr. Jack with his mules and wagons. He saw Captain Bob Lee at the store in Pilot Grove several times, and he told Mr. Dave that Captain Bob looked to him like he was a mighty fine gemm'an and a handsome man. Jim just didn't pay any attention to the stories he heard about killings and bad men on the road and Yankee soldiers on the lookout. He never had any trouble with anybody — Lees, Peacocks, Gentrys, Nances, Federal soldiers, freedmen, runaways — white and black, he liked them all. He wore his happy smile and trusted everybody as his friend.

If there was a big feud going on around him — like some folks said — Jim ignored it. He "jus' didn' take sides with nobody." As for that, neither did his "white folks," the Tates. First and last, that was hard to do in the gathering storm that was enveloping them.

CHAPTER 3

1867

Hidden Trails

BY THIS TIME BOB LEE HAD BUILT HIS HIDE-OUT
in the densest part of Wildcat Thicket. The place was dark
and sinister by day and well-nigh impenetrable by night.
It was hard by the Lee land and only a short gallop from
Bob's home. Now he spent more and more time there and
less and less at home. He could not forget that it was at
home he had been surprised and apprehended by the posse
of Union men who had taken him on a forced ride to
Choctaw Bottom. He didn't intend to let that happen again.

Lee's followers took pride in the safety of the Hide-out,
and boasted that it would never be discovered by Lee's ene-

mies. This little cove in the woods was on the order of an army tent; Bob made it himself, of good sturdy timber and black oilcloth which he boiled in linseed oil. This made it impervious to rain and sudden northers, and in the summers no other shelter than the low overhanging foliage of the underbrush was needed. It was closer to the ground than the regular army tent, making it necessary for Bob and his followers to crawl into the shelter.

As times became more perilous and life more dear, Lee and his men went underground. The hide-out became the perfect rendezvous where the general met and conferred with his most trusted lieutenants, and no general ever had more trustworthy men on his staff; there was not a traitor among them. His scouts and messengers included old men, farm wives, and teen-age girls and boys. One of the Dixon girls was said to have ridden many a mile on her fleet little pony carrying messages for Lee. If a stranger appeared in the community without good credentials, if any unusual incident or gathering occurred among the Union Leaguers, Lee knew it within an hour. There was never any lack of contact or communication. Although this was eighteen months after Appomattox, these folks diligently kept the flames of war hatreds and jealousies smouldering or blazing high all the time.

Lee's personality was one that fitted the period like a glove, whether of velvet or steel. His fiery, impetuous nature combined with the qualities of courage, gallantry, and daring, made him unquestionably the leader of the group seeking to restore the old order. Added to the above-named traits, he had great skill in firearms and the experience of four years of bitter fighting with Whitfield's Legion. He had physical strength, and a manner well-seasoned with chivalry. He loved his wife, Melinda, and so far as can be discovered, no other woman ever won his love. The loyalty of his women "subjects" was his to command, and there came times when they proved it.

The Union League, the party in power, openly stated it was the voice of the people, the champion of the freedmen, and the rulers of the new day. Its headquarters were, as might be expected, in the village of Pilot Grove. Its meetings were not held in any hidden cellar or any particular building or store. At any saloon, drugstore, blacksmith shop or even the Moss Hotel, members of the League could be found giving out opinions on what was going to happen now that the South had been defeated and Texas whipped to her knees. All their mutterings and prophecies might not have amounted to anything if they had not found a strong man for their leader. They found their man in Lewis Peacock. He was a big husky blonde with grey eyes, who had come to Texas from Kansas in the 1850's and had homesteaded a quarter-section of land on the Grayson-Fannin line lying about two miles east of Pilot Grove. Peacock's chief characteristic seems to have been ambition. The ownership of land gave him a terrific thirst for more. To own land, to be a leader in the community, to be the boss of local politics — these were the goals that enticed and inspired him. Certain it is that he had no taste for war. No record of any war service can be found, although he was of an age for fighting. He was forty-two in 1867 when he was beginning to cultivate a taste for political power.

During the war years there were many newcomers to the Corners, the majority being from Kansas, Missouri, Iowa, and other scattered points north and west. Some were well-to-do families who came for security reasons and tarried until the war was over. Others came with a view of staying if prospects were good. That usually meant if they could get some cheap land or easy money. Lewis Peacock made their acquaintances as soon as convenient and he could usually give them the information they wanted. It was natural that they sought his advice for he had so recently been one of them. He welcomed the Kansans, many of whom said they belonged to the Red Legs, an organization which had only two requisites for membership — loyalty to the Union, and skill in the use of the rifle and pistol. To the Missourians, who at home had been called Jay-hawkers, he gave assurance of homes and lands and jobs in Texas. He had come from Missouri himself and filed on his land in 1858, but he didn't pay it out until 1863. The 1860 census listed him as a wagon-maker and a native of North Carolina. From all accounts the wagon-maker was a practical opportunist with a quick sense of timing. He made one unfortunate and unforgettable statement, however, when he said that some day he meant to be the boss of all Grayson County! He kept his finger on the public pulse and could tell new settlers where land could be bought for two dollars an acre; if necessary, he could tell refugees and fugitives where safety could be found in the brush.

In this same year of mounting trouble, *The Jefferson Times and Republican* stated that 115,928 acres of land had been sold for taxes in Fannin County alone under an Act of the Legislature of 1866. If not redeemed within two years, owners' claims were to be barred. The destitute Southern owners became desperate in their efforts to hold their lands.

The Lees kept theirs, but that was because they had gold they had brought with them when they moved to Texas, said their Union foes. Now that times had become so perilous, old Daniel Lee had buried his pot of gold somewhere on the Lees' horse ranch. Bob Lee knew the spot, and so did one of his sisters, but no one else. The story of the hidden gold was circulated by the Union Leaguers and their friends and added more envy, hatred and resentment to the situation.

Peacock's place was near the Tate farm, and adjacent to that of Parson Gentry. There were times when the three families were very friendly and neighborly. Some of the parson's many children came over to play with Peacock's two children, John and Cathy. Peacock's wife was a likeable person; her name was Emmaline and she is listed in the census as a native of Florida. She and her husband had truly traveled a long trail from Florida and North Carolina through Tennessee to Missouri, Kansas and on to Texas to settle at the Corners.

Gradually members of Peacock's party began to be spoken of as Peacock's men; names like James Vaught, Jim Maddox, Hugh Hudson, John Baldock, some of the Nances, the Borens, and many others.

Likewise Lee's leaders (many of whom were relatives) were known to all: his brother-in-law, Parson Martin Smith, whose wife was Minerva Lee, was very close to the leader. His neighbors, the Dixons, were known and trusted by Captain Bob; there were hundreds of others, Confederates, farmers, merchants; Southerners all. Lines were sharply drawn by this time and it was hard to be neutral.

In the midst of all this politics, war, and feuding, there was still some thought given to schooling. Members of both parties wanted their children educated. That meant they had to hire a teacher. The prosperous Union folks could pay their share, but the poverty-stricken Southern landowners were unable to furnish any United States gold or greenbacks — and their Confederate money was worthless in exchange. Nevertheless, they managed to raise the salary when needed. They paid in kind — sometimes in eggs, butter, chickens, pigs, handwork, sewing, knitting. There were all sorts of ways, and several schools were kept going in the Four Corners area.

Dorinda Pierce was a young would-be teacher living in

Pilot Grove. Her family had come to Texas in 1859 from Sumner County, Tennessee, when Dorinda was eleven years old. Her father, Benjamin Pierce, was a veteran of the War of 1812, in which struggle he served as special courier to General Andrew Jackson. He was also closely related to the New England President of the United States in the 1850's — Franklin Pierce. The Benjamin Pierce family settled at Pilot Grove, and in a few years had established a reputation for learning and culture that made them respected by all parties. They were Southern in their sentiments, although they were not offensive or officious about it. They liked books to the extent that some people thought it srange how much time the Pierces could spend just reading. Dorinda had an eager, alert mind and seized every opportunity to stimulate it with study. She had received the finishing touches of her education at a seminary at Cannon, six miles west of Pilot Grove. The earnest young student decided to be a teacher, for she sensed that when men quit fighting they would school their children.

Her ambition was encouraged and enhanced by her older brother, Dr. William Hartwell Pierce, who was one of the best-liked physicians at the Corners. When the war ended he was thirty-one years old and living in the village of Pilot Grove with his wife and two children. He had much affection for his sister Dorinda and encouraged her in her ambitions to "do something" and "get somewhere," although he realized that few would do that in the first post-war years.

Dr. Pierce was well acquainted with members of the Peacock party and the Lee party. True to his Hippocratic oath, he never refused his services to anyone of either side, even though his affection was for the followers of Lee. Perhaps it was that very fact that pushed him rapidly toward his irresistible destiny — that of being the first victim of the war between the factions of Lee and Peacock. That year, when James W. Throckmorton, a citizen of Collin County, had just about reached the middle of his one and only hectic year as Governor of Texas, an incident occurred in Pilot Grove that sealed the doctor's doom. It was in the last week of February and one of those rare and beautiful days that forecast an early spring, when Bob Lee rode over to the village with some time to spend. What was the exact purpose of his trip to town is not known. Maybe he had no purpose other than a craving for the society of his fellows out in the open. Maybe he wanted to get information about his political enemies, the Peacock people, or maybe he came to spend some of the treasured Lee gold with the merchants of Pilot Grove. As Fate would have it, he was in a shop or grocery — no difference, the result would have been the same, for Bob Lee was never inconspicuous — when he met one of the higher-ups of the Peacock party face to face and the words began to fly. Nobody knows now, and it's doubtful if anybody knew then, whether the meeting was framed or accidental.

Fighting words about the "Red Legs," the freedmen, carpetbaggers, rebels, and many more of like ilk soon brought on a challenge to step outside and settle the argument. Then suddenly the Union Leaguer did an about-face. He brushed off his words with a laugh and offered his apologies to Lee. The gallant gesture was pleasing to the late Captain of the Confederacy and he turned to walk away. Just as he did so, a bullet grazed his ear and head and he fell to the ground, while his recent challenger put away his pistol and quickly turned his steps in another direction. Well for him that he wasted no time. There most certainly would have been more blood spilled, since friends of Lee rushed from every store, saloon and residence, to aid their stricken hero. In true Robin Hood style they surrounded him, vowing vengeance for the dastardly deed. Lee lay unconscious and apparently mortally wounded. Dr. Pierce was among those who had run forward at the sound of the shots. His home was nearby and he immediately ordered the men to carry Lee into his house for examination, giving no thought to the number of Peaccok men who might be watching him. His only aim at the moment was to give aid to a wounded man.

People waited outside for the doctor's report, and when it came from the doctor himself, there was joy among the Southerners. Lee was not dead; seriously wounded, said the "Doc," but it was possible to save him. A narrow escape, and he must not be moved for several days.

The news was flashed by messengers over the hidden trails that Bob Lee had been shot by Peacock men, but Dr. Pierce had saved him. Bob's wife, Melinda, came to nurse him. People in the thickets, in the villages, and on the farms, thought of little else.

A report went in to Austin to the Headquarters of the Fifth Military District under command of General John J. Reynolds, and the following entry was made in his ledger of: "Murder and Assaults with Intent to Kill." Listed as the criminals were James Maddox and John Vaught; listed as party injured — Robert Lee. The charge: "Assault with intent to murder." The result: "Set aside by the Military."

A few days later — while Lee was still convalescing in the Pierce home — a rider came up to Dr. Pierce's gate and gave the usual signal: "Hello! — hello!" The doctor came out to answer the call, but it was not a sick man who called him. Hugh Hudson, a Peacock follower, sat astride a handsome horse, dallying with a pistol in his belt. He'd just stopped, he 'lowed, to ask the Doc what he thought about the horse. He'd heard he'd made some remarks about it. The doctor was drawn into conversation about the terms of the horse trade and the ownership of the horse itself.

"You wouldn't be accusing me of horse stealing, would you, Doc?" asked Hudson, leaning forward and looking menacingly at the doctor in the waning twilight.

"That I would, Hudson," answered the valiant doctor. "You have named it; so you must agree with me. Good night." There was a movement of the horseman as the doctor turned from his gate. Before he had taken three steps there was a ringing shot, followed by the clattering hoof beats of the vanishing horse.

The doctor lay where he fell. Melinda and Dorinda ran into the yard, followed by the doctor's wife, Serena, and children, knowing full well what they should find. This time they carried him in the house and cared for his wound tenderly and stood by him solicitously after sending a rider for the doctor at Kentucky-town. Again the messages went out to the trails and the thickets. This time though no one could save the doctor, for the bullet had taken a deadly course. Three days later, on February 27, he was dead at thirty-three. Bob Lee suffered the agony of seeing the man who had saved his life die for his good deed.

With his own wounds still fresh, Lee swore to avenge the death of Dr. Pierce. So did others who esteemed the doctor and respected his skill. Many were heard to say: "The Union League must go!" Another report was sent to Austin for General Reynolds' records, which said: "Murder in the Corners of Hunt, Grayson, Collin and Fannin Counties" — and — "No action taken by the Military" — .

Thirty days after the doctor's death, *The McKinney Enquirer* stated: "We learn that a few days since two men called at the home of Bob Lee in the eastern part of the county (Collin), and after firing at him several times, made their escape thinking probably they had killed him. Lee, however, was not hurt. His brother arrived a little time after when the two traced the would-be assassins to Farmersville, and attacked them, killing one and wounding the other. We did not learn the names of the parties, or any particulars." And *The Dallas Herald* on March 30, revealed another incident in the fast-developing feud: "The body of a man about twenty years old and dressed in grey was found last week between Bonham and Kentucky-town. He is supposed to have committed suicide." Apparently, these two men went to their graves "unhonored, unwept, and unsung." Three men were dead in the month between February 27 and March 30; the first honored and respected, the others either unknown or their identities kept secret.

To three women — Dorinda Pierce, Serena Pierce, the doctor's wife, and Melinda Lee — death had struck close in the troublesome year of 1867.

CHAPTER 4

1868

No Quarter Given

MYSTERY AND MURDER WERE THE GALLOPING ghosts of '68, the twin dangers that plagued the unreconstructed state of Texas from border to border. In the vicinity of the Corners, the third year after Appomattox witnessed the rapid rise of lawlessness, an astonishing growth of bitterness among the people, and an increased friction between the Military and "popular desperadoes."

Like a raging fever, hatred spread from home to home; doors were locked, windows barred, rifles and pistols kept ready for instant use. The Iron-Clad Oath raised its hand and with the fury of an ugly ogre slapped the face of every

Confederate service man who dared to speak out for his rights in the "new days."

Immigrants and refugees from Kansas, Missouri, the Indian Nation, Iowa, and elsewhere, flocked into the Corners and crowded its little village of Pilot Grove to the bursting point. Nine out of ten of the newcomers sided with Lewis Peacock and his Union Leaguers, mainly because he held out bright promises of opportunities for participation in the reconstruction of Texas (along co-operative methods, yielding profits to all.)

On the other hand, the man in the hide-out in Wildcat Thicket did not forget how it all had come about. The murder of Dr. Pierce still hung over the Corners like a ghostly pall; to Bob Lee, its gloom was ever-present and sickening to the heart. He said as much in a letter to *The Bonham News,* in which he stated that Hudson was paid $300 to do the deed. One early report said that Hudson didn't want to kill the doctor; that he was really fond of him but that his vows to the Union League nullified his friendship.

The newspapers of the area were cautious but earnest in their efforts to report mysterious murders that followed the death of Dr. Pierce.

The *Greenville Gladiator* had aptly reported one incident with — "Lee and his party of six met Taber and his party of three at Farmersville — a fight ensued."

This report pin-pointed the situation that all men carried guns, and whenever one group met another group 'a fight ensued," with death as the reward for some before the fight ended. The civil authorities seldom made either inquiry or investigation; neither did the Military, other than to send a report to Headquarters at Austin, although the entire area was under martial law. The ghosts of vengeance diligently meted out justice to all.

Hugh Hudson met his Nemesis in the early part of the year. His avengers caught up with him at some mysterious rendezvous where rival groups met on starless nights. One story said he was shot by Lee and his men in his home vicinity of the Corners; another said that when Hudson fled the country he was followed by Lee men and shot somewhere in East Texas; still another said he died in camp on the Jefferson Road from wounds sustained in a battle with Lee's men.

Dr. W. C. Holmes, who became Dr. Pierce's successor, staunchly believed the last-named story and had good reason for his theory. Holmes was a young Mississippi physician who had landed in the Corners in April, 1867, just two months after the shooting of Dr. Pierce. Notwithstanding the stories he heard of killings, shootings, and even pitched battles, he liked the place and decided to stay. He took up quarters in the village of Pilot Grove and took over Dr. Pierce's practice.

By the end of the year he had done so well that he made his plans to return to Mississippi for his bride. He set out in early Januray, 1868, traveling by stage over the well-known route to Jefferson. The first overnight camp was at Saltillo in Hopkins County. There the incident occurred that gave him his theory about the death of Hudson.

Saltillo was a regular stop for stages, teamsters, wagoners, and solitary travelers as well. That night found the usual number of people in the village. Campfires were numerous and in the main room of the inn a roaring log fire gave out a welcome warmth, for the weather was cool and crisp in early January.

After supper the doctor was standing near the fireplace chatting with a fellow-traveler going east. The "Doc" never wasted an opportunity of exchanging opinions with his fellow man wherever he found him, but he had hardly got his argument started when the front door creaked open slightly and a voice spoke from outside.

"Ain't you the new doc from Pilot Grove?"

"I reckon you might call me that, friend," replied Dr. Holmes. "I took Dr. Pierce's place."

"That's what I thought. Well, you might be interested to know a man from the Grove just died in our camp, down the road a piece." The speaker was still not visible.

"Certainly, I'm interested. Maybe I know him. Who is it?" The doctor's curiosity was characteristic of his personality.

"We got him laid out in our wagon bed. Want to see him? It's Hugh Hudson."

The sputtering of the log fire sounded like echoing rifle fire to the men who heard the name Hugh Hudson. However, the doctor triumphed over the momentary silence created by the mention of the name of Hudson and spoke out bravely: "My friend, if you'll just tell me who you are and where the body is, I'll gladly follow you and —"

The voice outside made no answer, but the door was pushed open and a lighted lantern was upraised as a signal. The doctor stepped outside and followed the swinging lantern down the road. He tried other questions, but could get no answers from his guide. After about a quarter of a mile they stopped at a low-burning campfire, and by this additional light the doctor decided that the man with the lantern was a teamster he had occasionally seen at Pilot Grove; perhaps that was only because he wanted to believe he had seen the man before, and had not come merely because of the name Hugh Hudson.

Another voice spoke from beyond the campfire. "Take a fast look, Doc; we're going to give him a quick burying right away." The man with the lantern moved forward to a nearby wagon and motioned with his upraised arm to the

34

doctor. Holmes stepped forward and looked closely at the body of the man in the wagon bed. He had never seen Hugh Hudson in life so he could not swear this was the right man, although the general appearance seemed to fit the descriptions he had heard of Hudson. The doctor had the uneasy feeling that this was exactly why he had been brought here; to corroborate the death of Hudson on some future occasion.

Doctor Holmes wondered if the man to be buried so hastily at Saltillo was the real Hugh Hudson, and if the man with the lantern and the man at the campfire were Lee's men finishing a job they had been sent to do; or Peacock's men taking care of a member of their clan. The doctor asked no questions for he knew he would get no answers.

Hudson's death ocurred in January, and by February it was already catalogued with the past. A fresher murder absorbed the attention of both parties. This time there was no doubt of its being friend against friend.

Elijah Clark was a young man who consorted with both parties, but more frequently with Peacock and his Union Leaguers than with members of the Lee clan. However, he liked the Dixon family — Lee followers, and in particular, Clark liked Hester Anne, the oldest of the Dixon girls. It so happened that young Clark met his death because of this admiration for Hester Anne.

Clark rode up to the Dixon home one day to ask Hester to go to a party with him. It was late February or early March and spring was opening up so enchantingly that a few people were allowing themselves to think about purely social gatherings. Lige knew that the Dixons did not look upon him with favor because of his politics, but he relied upon his childhood friendship for protection — a dangerous thing to do in feuding times.

He dismounted at the front gate, threw his bridle reins

carelessly over the picket fence, and strolled towards the house, calling loudly: "Hester Anne!"

She answered by coming to the door and inviting him in. Lige carefully took his pistol out of its holster and laid it on the table in the hall as proof that this was a friendly call. But when Hester said "no" and he failed to obtain his objective, the social factor disappeared.

In high dudgeon he stalked out of the house and immediately encountered his old chum, William Dixon, called Billy by his intimates. Young Dixon had just tethered his own horse to the same picket fence and was hurrying in to see who the visitor might be; he knew the horse but he didn't know whether it would be Lige who had ridden him there.

In a sudden fit of pique at being scorned by Hester Anne, and consequently by all her family, and likewise by the Lee Clan, young Clark, when he reached the fence, grabbed a pistol from the holster of Billy's horse and turned and fired a reckless shot in the direction of his former friend. Still retaining the pistol, he jumped upon his own horse and turned to gallop away; but he had made a fatal mistake.

Billy Dixon was quick with his answer. Infuriated by what appeared to be the treachery of his friend, he turned and seized Clark's pistol forgotten by its owner and still resting on the hall table. Running outside, Billy fired one shot at the fleeing horseman.

Ironic tragedy engulfed him as Lige Clark fell; killed by his own pistol in the hands of his boyhood playmate. Dixon was young, hot-headed and reckless, but he aged greatly in a matter of minutes. Despair gripped the teen-aged brother and sister as they saw the deplorable result of a social call that was bound to fan the smouldering hatred of the Union Leaguers and draw tauter the safety net around their leader in Wildcat Thicket.

In less than a month Billy Dixon met death in a fiendish manner. It happened on the main highway of commerce — the Jefferson Road. Jack Dixon started one of his wagons to Jefferson with a load of cotton; he put Billy, and his young cousin, Charlie, in charge. Following the usual custom, the boys were to haul cotton on the down trip and household goods and supplies on the return trip. It was toward the end of March and the weather was turning warm. Billy was sixteen, and Charlie only a few years older; consequently, the boys set out with high spirits and a feeling of gratitude toward Jack Dixon for giving them this business trip by themselves.

Unfortunately, their plans were known to their enemies, the Union League men. The Dixon boys had journeyed only about twenty miles when they stopped to make repairs on one of their wagon wheels. Billy took a handful of nails and a hammer and as he knelt to inspect the wheel, a posse of a dozen men suddenly appeared and surrounded the wagon, demanding the boys' surrender. They had evidently been following the wagon, keeping out of sight in the brush along the road. The trouble with the wagon gave them an opportunity to accomplish their purpose much sooner than they had expected. The boys had no time to get their guns out of the wagon.

"It's the Red Legs, Charlie. We're in for it, They're Peacock's men," warned Billy as the possemen drew closer.

Perhaps they heard young William's warning; perhaps they didn't, but they dismounted swiftly and while two of them seized Charlie, who was standing at the front of the wagon holding the lines of the mule team, the others grabbed Billy still kneeling with the nails in his hands. They informed him that he was to be granted a quick court-martial. It is not known whether there were military men in the posse, but such was not at all uncommon. Federal soldiers were quartered at Greenville, Bonham, and Sherman. The Union League relied upon them for their protection, and League leaders made it a practice to report rumors, fugitives, and what they called "resistance to civil authority." Since according to Charlie's story, as it was later reported, Union League men were in the posse, it is possible that they had sent to Greenville for a detail of soldiers to run down a fugitive and breaker of the law who was known to be a member of the Lee Gang.

At any rate, the so-called court-martial decided speedily that any man or boy who followed Bob Lee deserved the death sentence. The country would be better off without him. For some unknown reason they did not place Charlie under arrest. He was a Dixon but they knew he was only a cousin of the Dixons at the Mound, whereas Billy's father, mother, brothers, and sisters were quick to carry out Lee's commands, run his errands, and take his messages to and from Wildcat Thicket. They centered on young William; he was too close to the Chief for their own safety.

"Where you think you're going?"

"Jefferson, with our cotton."

"Dangerous business for Lee's men to be on the public road, young fellow. Didn't you know that? We can he'p you out. We can take you off the road. Tie him up, boys!"

It would be neither right nor just to give a Lee man an easy death; a guerrilla's death the hard way was better. Ropes were handy; quickly and expertly Billy was tied to his wagon wheel. The next step was to scare the mules into running away. With ropes and switches from the trees, and boards from the wagon, they beat upon the mules and screamed at them and cursed them, but the mules refused to budge. They took upon themselves the nature of their lowly kinsmen, the donkeys, and declined to move. Either they were used to such carryings-on or they waited for the voice of their master.

Such action by the mules angered the possemen more than ever. With a snip of the knives they loosened Billy and told him to march ten paces with hands up. They drew nearer with rifles cocked to quicken his pace. Five paces, six, seven; a single bullet split the air and Billy slumped in his tracks.

Possemen mounted again. "Accidental, Charlie, somebody's rifle must have slipped. Better get him home to Jack." Clattering hooves sounded their retreat to the west. They would reach the Corners first and give their own report.

Charlie raced forward and dropped beside his cousin. "Bill! Bill! Did they get you?" Silence gave the answer. No need to hurry now. Stunned and heart-broken, the boy sat there, unconscious of the passing time and his stinging tears, until voices awakened him.

"What's the matter, young feller? Be ye in trouble?" They were two men riding toward the Corners. They dismounted and offered their help. Whether they were active followers of Lee or not they didn't say, but they were friendly and they knew the Dixons. Without any more questions or answers, they helped Charlie with his mournful task, then tied their horses to the back of the wagon, took the lines of the Dixon team and headed toward Dixon's Mound.

The story of the unwarranted attack on the two teenagers set off new waves of hatred. Charlie's report that Peacock's men had been in the posse incensed the members of Lee's party. The leader himself when he heard it was embittered more than ever because the Dixons had been among his closest followers, and it pained him to think that Jack Dixon's young son had become a victim of that friendship. It was dangerous to follow Lee.

The newspapers were cautious in reporting these murders, skirmishes and ambush attacks. Added to their caution were inaccuracies. *The Dallas Herald* stated in its issue of May 2, 1868: "If our citizens would take an interest in reporting all items of interest as they transpire in their immediate neighborhood we would be able to give a correct account but it is impossible for us on mere rumor to give accurate reports." Their comment was proved by the account in the *McKinney Messenger* of the killing of Billy Dixon. Says *The Messenger*: "Two men, Dickson and Clark, were killed on Saturday last, March 28th, near the upper edge of Collin County by a party of soldiers who had been sent from Sherman to arrest them. One resisted and was killed; the other attempted to escape and was shot down." There was some truth in the newspapers account — Dixon was killed, not while resisting arrest or attempting to escape, but in cold blood. Clark was already dead a month or so before, at the hands of the same young Billy Dixon.

It was to be expected that the Lee clan would seek revenge for the death of Dixon, after the mourning subsided and Billy had been safely buried. Then rumors were rife, tempers were short, and nights — as well as days — were dangerous. Plans had to be perfected in the greatest secrecy. For another month and one-half there were no known murders, raids, or skirmishes.

Then it happened. In mid-May at the Nance farm there was a meeting in which three men were killed. One report says that Peacock and some of his followers had a meeting scheduled at the Nance farm; at night, of course, in the dark of the moon. The Nances had a big horse-lot and it was there the meeting took place. Dow Nance, a son of the family, had thrown in his lot with the Peacock men. The Sanders brothers — Dan and Clay — were there, so was John Baldock, close friend of Dow Nance. Lee and a posse of his men made a raid on the horse-lot. Unknown messengers had carried correct reports to Wildcat Thicket. A big fight took place just outside the Nance corral. No Lee people were hurt, but after they rode away in victory and Peacock counted his men, it was found that two men lay dead — Dow Nance and John Baldock — and Dan Sanders appeared to be fatally wounded; others suffered minor wounds, including Peacock himself. This was his second time to escape by a hair the accuracy of Lee's rifles.

Another version of this affray at the Nance Corral has it that Peacock and his men rode north from the corral to an unknown rendezvous and were attacked from ambush en route. This legend says that Lee rode at the head of his posse and gave orders to his men to remember that Peacock was his target and his only. He almost finished the Union leader that night. It was Peacock's horse that saved him. It swerved in the nick of time and Peacock, though seriously and painfully wounded, turned the horse into the deep brush and lived to ride another night.

Young Dan Sanders died from his wounds, and Baldock and Nance were buried in one grave in the old Mt. Carmel cemetery west of Desert Creek.

This time there was weeping at the parson's home; pretty Mary Anne Gentry, who had married Dow Nance, was momentarily expecting her first child.

As soon as he was sufficiently recovered from his wounds, Peacock called in his men for a council. He evidently resolved to bring matters to a head and to appeal direct to the top brass of the Fifth Military District, General Reynolds himself at Austin. Another one of those inaccurate rumors began to circulate that Peacock had reported the Nance affair and that more Federal troops would soon be sent to the Corners.

The Red Legs of Kansas moving into North Texas had become an important part of Peacock's organization. Back in Kansas they had been a reputable law-enforcement body, with only two requirements for membership: Loyalty to the Union cause, and skill in the use of the rifle and pistol. They wore red leggings as an insignia of their clan and from this took their name. They were bitterly hated by the Confederate guerrillas and the latter's sympathizers in Kansas and Missouri. In the aftermath of the war, when they came to Texas, it was the same. Those who moved into the Corners became the local henchmen for Peacock. They carried out his orders in their own manner, which meant they threw in a lot of offensive red tape to show their power. They were even called Hogskins, because they stole hogs, skinned them, took the meat and left the skins on the roadside, in the barns, or on the field, as the occasion demanded. Wherever a pig or hog showed itself, it was taken. Petty thievery, robbery, and pillaging increased, and all of it was ascribed to the Red Legs, doing the bidding of the Union League.

Capt. Bob Lee, the hero hiding in Wildcat Thicket, was not without recourse. He, too, resolved to make an appeal — there was only one way he could make it, and that was through a letter to the press. *The Texas State News*, published at Bonham, was well-liked by the citizens of the four counties because they felt the editor was fair to both sides. It was in June 1868, about a month or six weeks after the Nance affray, that Bob Lee wrote his famous letter to the editor. It was the one time he gave his story to the public, and it reflects the gallantry and courage of the Southern soldier. He was not afraid to call names; perhaps he wanted the records of time to show how the feud started. Whatever his motive, the letter has added to his fame, and it proved a powerful weapon at the time. Why not? Read it here in part:

Lee Station, Fannin County
June 26, 1868

Editor Texas News:

If you will permit me the use of your valuable columns

42

I would like to give you a true statement of what is known as the Pilot Grove Difficulty, notwithstanding there has been no killing in Pilot Grove at all except Dr. Pierce. But to begin:

I was raised in this state, and enlisted in the Southern army, and fought the best I could, until the surrender when I laid down my arms and returned home to live, as I thought, in peace the balance of my life. But how badly I was disappointed you will soon see.

A short time after my arrival home, one night when I was sick in bed, I was arrested by a party of men: (Israel Boren, Lewis Peacock, James Maddox (?), Bill Smith, Sam Bier, and Hardy Dial) wearing the U. S. uniform, and was told by them that I would be carried to Sherman to stand trial for offenses committed during the war. Of course, I surrendered and was perfectly willing to yield myself. After we had proceeded a short distance from my home another party (in civilian dress) fell in with us. Among these citizens I recognized a party known as 'Doc' Wilson and several other thieves. Well, as we proceeded to Sherman, 'Doc' Wilson began to hint to me that I should buy out and not go to Sherman. Now, you can imagine my dismay, when our entire party, U.S. Soldiers and all, halted in Choctaw Bottom this side of Sherman, went off the road and stationed a guard over me apparently with a view of staying some time, in the meantime 'Doc' Wilson still persuading me to buy out and escape the punishment at Sherman, which he presented as very severe. I repeatedly begged to be taken to Sherman; sick, hardly able to sit up (and a) surrounded man. Now then I was in Choctaw Bottom, surrounded by a band of thieves. After keeping me thirty-six hours, my sickness growing worse all the time and I (still) begging them to take me to Sherman, I finally agreed to accept their offer and obtain my release. I agreed to give them my mule, saddle and bridle, a $20-dollar gold piece which I had in my pockets, and executed my note to 'Doc' Wilson with my father's name for security for $2000 in gold payable on demand, and promised to leave the country forever. Having no pen and ink, Wilson made a pen of a toothpick and ink of gunpowder and water mixing it in my brother's hand. (He came with me when arrested).

Now, after being arrested, I thought to try the civil law on these scoundrels, and to prevent me from doing so they have ever since tried to kill me.

One day — about twelve after this (arrest) — I was in Pilot Grove and met Jim Maddox (a friend of Peacock's), and I told him that if he desired to fight me I would loan him a pistol, but the coward said he didn't want to hurt me and proposed taking a drink, saying he was sorry he had done what he did. After drinking with him, I told him I wanted to be let alone, and he said all right. However, he went out of the grocery store, borrowed a pistol from a friend, slipped up behind me while I was making a contract with a Negro to do some work, and shot me in the face. He then left me on the ground for dead, and bragged that he (had) shot Bob Lee's brains out. I was in a very precarious condition for some time and would have perished but for the timely aid and skill of the late Dr. Pierce. I may add here that the excellent gentleman (soon after my recovery) was called to his gate and brutally murdered in the presence of his family by one of the clan — Hugh Hudson. The doctor's death is attributed to his kindness in taking care of me in his house and nursing me.

Still the civil authorities (took) no notice of these things. I have done everything I could to procure peace; I have even tried to buy it with money; and I have done every way in my power to do right and be peaceable; still I am hunted by a squad of U. S. soldiers, assisted by a number of horse thieves who come to my house, throw fire in the beds, drag my children by their feet across the floor and insult my wife. Yet, the U. S. troops stood by and said not a word.

* * *

Now I will not cease to punish these men so long as I can find them. Peacock still hires men to kill me and they must take the consequences. — I am willing to surrender myself to any impartial civil authority at any time, but will not give myself up, unarmed, to thieves and robbers.

I am sorry to take so much of your valuable time and space, but a great many people, including the Military, have no idea of the true origin of all this trouble, so I give you all the particulars. I remain yours,

Robert Lee

Lee's popularity reached a new high after this. It forced Peacock to write to Austin again for more help, and finally, on August 27, General J. J. Reynolds issued his famous proclamation putting a price on Lee's head by offering one thousand dollars reward for "anyone who would deliver Bob Lee to the Post Commander at Marshall or Austin." The former Brevet Major Reynolds had just been made a brigadier and placed in command of the Fifth Military District, which now consisted of Texas alone, with State Headquarters at Austin.

It was during this same summer of '68 that a new judge for the Seventh Judicial District was appointed by the Military. Hardin Hart, of Greenville, was described by Chas. De Morse in his *Clarksville Standard* as "six-four in his stockings and a cow-hunter before the war."

The *Denton Monitor* in its issue of August 5th, '68, announced that " — Judge Hardin Hart has opened a military court at Pilot Grove, where he will proceed to try before a corporal's drum-head all offenders against the people of the 7th Judicial District. Hear, O, all ye sinners and tremble!" And a little later, in the issue of September 12, the *Monitor* said: "General Reynolds, commander of Texas, has sent Lt. Vernon of his staff on a visit through the counties of North Texas to inquire into the state of affairs and learn whether or not the civil law can be enforced."

Perhaps Lee's letter to the *State News*, with its accusations against both military and civil authorities, saying that neither side would enforce the laws of the land, created this activity. General Reynolds began to give out bulletins. On October 3 he reported that: "the condition of things in Texas is incredible to citizens of other states, and a disgrace to the civilization of the age."

On October 17, Judge Hardin Hart asked permission to hold extra sessions of the District Court in Grayson, Fannin, and Hunt Counties. Ol' Hardened Hart, as he was known, always traveled with a military escort, and his court sessions were full of horseplay, if nothing more, said some.

In the meantime, Lt. Chas A. Vernon, U. S. 4th Cavalry, turned in his report to General Reynolds on conditions in North Texas. On the 19th of October he wrote in part: "Bob Lee seems to be the most popular man in this section of the country — citizens would give him all the aid in their power, also with force of arms if necessary."

That was not a bright report for the General, and his views of the uncivilized state of affairs in Texas grew gloomier daily. He dispatched a detachment of troops under command of Lt. Sands, with orders to bring in Lee and end the squabble in Northeast Texas. The lieutenant, according to his military reports, had at all times a portion of his command under a non-com officer lying in the brush with the strong hope that they would eventually capture their man. They put out that they were surrounding Lee's Thicket and had Lee on the defensive.

In a way, they were right. Lee *was* on the defensive more than he had yet been. He never slept at his home any more; in fact he never emerged from his hide-out in the Thicket until one of his family had made sure it was safe to do so. Captain Bob knew somebody would be trying to collect that one-thousand dollar reward.

In December, said the press: "A U. S. soldier was killed near Farmersville. He was one of a squad in search of Bob Lee, guided by one L. Peacock — ".

The tempestuous and turbulent year drew to a close with battle lines well-drawn; Lee and Peacock still safe, but with that margin of safety growing increasingly more dangerous.

CHAPTER 5

1869

Blood Flows Freely

IN THE EFFORT TO STABILIZE THAT LINE OF safety, much blood was to be shed in the new year of 1869; bloody trails were to checkerboard the area of Four Corners with their gory stains extending east to Marshall, south to Dallas, west to Gainesville, and north into the Indian Nation. In January, it was disclosed that the state that had repulsed all attempts at invasion by Northern troops in the late war, was now garrisoned by one hundred companies of Federal soldiers. Law and order were represented by a dual-control system of Civil Authority and Military Authority. Decisions of the former could easily be set aside by the latter, from which there was no appeal.

MURDER AT THE CORNERS

General J. J. Reynolds, from his headquarters in Austin, dispatched his blue boys hither and yon about the state. It irked him no little that he was constantly having to send men to Northeast Texas and the trouble spot of the Corners. His Special Order No. 16 offering a liberal reward for the capture of Bob Lee, had remained unclaimed.

As a matter of fact, the citizenry resented the presence of the Yankees they had fought so desperately for four years to keep out, and any appointee by the Military to a Civil post was mistrusted and looked upon with contempt. Hardin Hart was such an appointee. He was a Union sympathizer, and when he was named judge of the 7th Judicial District, he immediately became unpopular with the citizens of the trouble-zone — Grayson, Fannin, Collin and Hunt. As a precautionary measure, Judge Hart established the custom of traveling to his court sessions with a military escort, consisting usually of sixteen enlisted men, commanded by a non-commissioned officer or lieutenant. The escort was often called the "Judge's life-preservers and body-minders" by both press and public. His "minders" went everywhere with him. There was one time, however, when he appeared in McKinney for a court session two days ahead of his escort and *The Messenger* immediately reported the judge's arrival by saying the "Judge was looking as if he were able to drink enough rot-gut to turn an overshot mill wheel all summer."

Judge Hart was a Greenville man, and was described by the *Greenville Herald* as a man with "a good heart, a clear head, and much honesty." This description was said by *The Bonham News* to be "a good joke on Hardin." The *News* also, in another issue early in the year, indignantly protested the after-effects of one of Judge Hart's court sessions in the Fannin County capital by saying: "Hardin and his body-minders ought to have been put in the lock-up for making their gallant charge upon our courthouse yard and tearing down our courtyard fence, destroying our shrubbery, making a pony-corral out of our well-shed, and a horse-lot out of the courthouse yard." The *News* was the most outspoken of the area papers and did not hesitate to give out its pungent comments on every topic of the day, great or small.

McKinney at this time boasted two newspapers, the *Enquirer* and *The Messenger*. The *Enquirer,* under the management of Captain Bingham, was much more Southern in its sentiments than *The Messenger.* The papers of Bonham and McKinney were strongly pro-Southern and had been so from the first days of the war; they were ardent secessionists. The majority of citizens in these two towns felt the same way.

Sherman had its *Courier* and Greenville its *Herald,* which were pro-Union in policy. Grayson County citizens had voted against secession in '61, and there were many Republicans in the county. At Greenville the Union troops maintained their headquarters for the area and consequently the *Herald* "puffed up the boys in blue," according to the Bonham *News.*

The press of the four counties reflected the discontent, the feeling of injustice (that had been done,) and (also) the determination to regain their former independence. In this year of stress and strain, gun-battles, and posses, these editors often printed flippant quips, and took sharp cracks at the customs of the day and the cheap politics of the Pease administration at Austin.

On March 20, 1869, the *Sherman Courier* printed what it called "A Market Report" which read as follows:

BREAD STUFFS	Rising every day
GUNPOWDER	Goes off easily
BEER	Shows a downward tendency
INDIGO	The trade is dying
PICKLED PORK	Dead and very inactive

BRANDY	Very spirited
VERMILLION	Finds a red-dy sale
NUTMEGS	In greater demand
LEAD	Very heavy

Another Market Report of another issue in sober prose quotes the price of eggs as ten cents per dozen and butter as twelve cents per pound. Cotton and coffee were the same, namely: eighteen cents per pound.

In January the *Courier* asked the Legislature, then in session at Austin, to change the name of Grayson County to Pease County. E. M. Pease was serving as Governor by military appointment, and his sentiments were said to be Northern. This was meant no doubt as a slap at the Northerners of Grayson County. The *Courier's* request was coldly received by some, but mostly it was good for a laugh and a joke. The other papers printed comments from its readers; some said that if such a change were made, then the name of Sherman should be changed to Carpet-Bag City, this being a name more appropriate to the sentiments of its citizens.

Taxes of every kind plagued all the citizens of the area, and the *Bonham News* printed an unsigned poem entitled *"We're Taxed"*, in one of its January issues. Its doggerel verse expressed truthfully the economic mood of Texans in Reconstruction. The same out-spoken editor may have been the author.

WE'RE TAXED

We're taxed upon our clothing, boys.
Upon our meat and bread;
Our carpets and our dishes, boys,
Our table and our bed.

Our coffee, tea and lights, my boys,
Are taxed with all the rest,
And if we do but murmur, boys,
They'll say 'It's so assessed.'

We're taxed upon our mortgage, boys,
Our checks, our notes and bills,
Upon our deeds and contracts, boys,
Upon our trusts, and wills.

We're taxed upon our whiskey, boys,
Upon our stores and shops,
Our barrels and our stoves, boys,
Upon our brooms and mops.

We're taxed for our physic, boys,
And if we should but die
We're tax-ed for the coffins
In which we then must lie.

We're taxed on everything, my boys,
Which God in mercy's given.
Yes, even on the Bible, boys,
That points the way to Heav'n.

In another issue the editor rhapsodized over the construction of a bridge over Bois d' Arc Creek, the connecting link between Fannin and Grayson Counties:

Let bugles to the trumpets toot,
And fifes in spasms squeal it,
Let howling drums in anthems hoot,
And creaking anvils peal it!
The Bridge is finished!
Yes, Bois d'Arc, that meanest, boggiest, stickiest,
bottomlessest, infernalest hole this side of the
regions of Inferno is no longer a dread and a terror.
This is the grandest achievement of the age —
RECONSTRUCTION NOT EXCEPTED!

51

MURDER AT THE CORNERS

The editors of *The News* — Tom Burnet and W. T. Gass, Jr. — possessed a keen sense of humor and by their witticisms sought to boost the morale of their readers and enable them to laugh off their troubles; they appealed to civic pride and boasted that their city had 3000 people in '69 with two private schools — one advertised as the Bonham High School with a tuition at $1.50 to $3.50 per month, and the other, the up-and-coming college labeled Carlton Male and Female Seminary. In January, the entire city awaited anxiously the arrival of a monster bell for the seminary; ordered out of New York by Professor Carlton, the bell was said to weigh 500 pounds, and *The News* asked: "What city in Texas can rank Bonham in the way of a bell?" In a later issue they spoke out for the organization of a brass band in these words: "If the village of Pin Hook (Paris) has tooters, no reason why Bonham should not, too."

But when it came to expressing opinions on the gun-battles going on between the posses of the Military-Civilian authorities and the popular so-called desperadoes, the editors skirted the fringe of opinion; however, with a good deal of subtlety they kept their readers informed, and even hinted their own support of the desperadoes. For example, on Saturday, January 23, 1869, they asked: "Where is the man that caught Hardin-ed Hart having a secret social chat with Bob Lee, the desperado, during Court Week? We are told there *is* such a man. Bring him up!"

This challenge of course was never met, but it did reflect the general talk that Bonham was Lee's town; that he had been in town that week, and that ol' Hardened Hart would follow a hands-off policy with Lee.

It was obvious that underneath this raillery of the press there lurked the bogy of Yankee rule; its power was increasing daily as General Reynolds, and then General Canby, sent more and more troops to Northeast Texas. As a result of this policy, the Union League with its friends and sympathizers continued their attacks on Southerners. Such a situation made desperadoes of men who had been Secessionists and Southern soldiers.

In a January issue the editors of the same *News* reported a murder in the briefest possible terms: "The body of a murdered man was found in the south part of Grayson County. His death was caused by two gunshot wounds — one in the right side, the other in the head."

As to the attacks on Southerners, a news item reported succinctly: "Daniel Lee, father of Bob Lee, was robbed and otherwise mistreated by a party of thirty men who came to his house looking for his son."

In January, another murdered man was discovered in a small community south of Sherman. The victim was well-known in the community and feeling mounted quickly because of the brutal manner in which the man had been killed. Robbery appeared to have been the motive. This time the Military acted quickly; a posse of civilian and military rode out of Sherman twenty-five miles south to a farmhouse five miles north of McKinney. Here they arrested two young men hiding in the farmhouse and took them to the Sherman jail, where they were to spend the next two, and last, months of their lives. They had come to Texas less than six months ago with the expectations of gaining great money and fortune, but had found the state in such a state of confusion that they soon accepted the theory of "Take it where you find it!" John Thompson and William Blackmore were the two young men now shackled in chains on the charge of murder. Their trial was set for the first Monday in February in the District Court before Judge Hart.

The best legal talent available was employed on both sides for the trial; the verdict of the jury was: "Guilty of murder in the first degree." Judge Hardened Hart pronounced the death sentence and named March 26 as the day of execution. For the next eight weeks the men were to be kept under close guard and weighted with heavy chains.

According to the story printed in *The Sherman Courier*, Thompson was the older of the two and also the instigator and promoter of the crimes committed by the two. Blackmore wrote a farewell letter to his mother in Missouri, in which he pleaded with her not to allow his younger brother to come to Texas — "Don't give your consent for him to come, Ma, for this country is in an awful state of affairs. It is overrun with outlaws. He is young and liable to be led astray. At home with you is the place for him to be.

"I was doing well until this came up. I was farming in Collin County, Texas, when a gentleman from Missouri by the name of Thompson, came to where I was living and I took him in as a partner. He was a man of fine appearance; he proposed to me several depredations. I at last consented to go with him. He persuaded me not to work for a living — that there was an easier way to get it. O, that I had never seen him!

From your dying son,
W. O. B."

The hanging on March 26 was made a great spectacle and was witnessed by people from the four-counties area. The scaffold and gallows were erected on the east side of the square. "The day dawned beautiful and clear," says *The Courier*. "By ten A. M. the square was filled with visitors. The hanging took place at 1 P. M. The prisoners were led out enshrouded in white. Blackmore appeared quiet and resigned; Thompson in stern determination. Neither spoke but Thompson was sterner and harder in appearance. Blackmore's death was instantaneous from a broken neck, but Thompson's death was prolonged for 30 minutes of agony.

"The Rev. W. P. Petty was with them on the scaffold and gave the final prayer for them. Mr. Petty also, while with them on the scaffold, read the dying declaration of each."

These "dying declarations" were in the form of letters to the public. They were printed in *The Courier* and afterward copied in most of the papers of Texas. They are long letters full of much detail, but there is a vividness about them and a tone of truth that makes them bear another reprint today. Here is a portion of John Thompson's letter:

"I am to die today and my sentence is just. I desire to live for life is sweet; and I can't say I am afraid to die but I am not *willing* to die. As I pass off before you, however, and join the uncounted company beyond the flood, I desire to administer a warning to the young men of my country.

"I have lived long enough to attest from my own expedience that a man's circumstances are inexorable and that they make him what he is. No man is independent of the company he keeps; he may vainly think so, but before he is aware of it, that company, be it good or bad, has moulded him into its own image. While yet a boy I mingled in bad company and I can see now that my mind and morals took on a bias that like the hand of unyielding destiny has led me to this sad and solemn hour of my profitless history. I played at cards and soon was led into gambling, and I took the social glass with my friends. — It grew into a habit with me, and not infrequently I was wildly intoxicated — I have lived a wild and wicked life. After the war I went back home to Missouri, but I was pursued and driven away from home, from political differences and private prejudices I could not live there in peace. I then came to Texas thinking I would make this state my home. I had been in your state but a short time when I aided in the commission of the crime for which I am to die. I do believe that a man's sins, sooner or later, bloodhound-like will scent him up and hunt him down. I have been running in sin a long time but it has overtaken me at last.

"And now, young men, as I turn from you to die, let me beseech you to avoid drinking, swearing, Sabbath-breaking and gambling, the sins which first started me down the hill of crime. I pray you do not send your personal hatreds into the grave after me.

"My friends, a kind but long farewell!

John Thompson"

Blackmore's "dying declaration," as read by the Rev. Petty from the scaffold, confesses his part in the murder for which he is to die, "but before I *do* die," says Blackmore, "I want to say a few words to the young men of my country as a warning to them. In my childhood my parents taught me my duty to God and man. I was a good boy up to my 15th year, when I went into the Confederate army. Unfortunately for me, I went into a company of very wicked men; they were my companions, and step by step I imitated their example, until I committed the crime that brought me here. Young men, if you keep wicked, profane, drinking, gambling, company you will certainly rush to ruin too! The difference between you and me is — you are looking *forward* upon life and I am looking *backward* upon it. I can see danger where some of you do not see it, and with my last breath I warn you to keep good company or none —.

"And now, my friends. my time has come and I wave you the kindest farewell! Wm. O. Blackmore."

In this dramatic manner ended the story of the great hanging. The executions created a legend that lingered in the Red River Valley. The names of Thompson and Blackmore were mentioned again and again by the Unionists as examples of law enforcement in the days of Reconstruction. Yet these men were not members of either the Lee or Pea-

cock party. Their crimes were not due to politics; neither
were they known as Unionists or Red Legs; in fact, they
were not even Texans, except for a few months. They were
Missourians and had served in the Confederate Army — (at
least Blackmore says so, and Thompson implies so) and were
so beset by the conditions in southern Missouri that they
sought escape in Texas, the same routine followed by many
people at the close of the war when G T T became the
popular phrase. "Gone to Texas" brought good fortune to
some and ill to others.

Some Southerners in their frenzy called these men "scalawags" and "bushwhackers," but incorrectly so, for those two
opprobrious titles were applied to men who hid out in the
brush to escape military service. Thompson and Blackmore
were more like Quantrell's Guerrillas or Anderson's men
than any other of the types that flooded Texas during and
just after the war. Thompson and Blackmore came from the
same part of Missouri as Quantrell and Anderson and could
have been members of their band, although never acknowl-
edging it or even implying it. Whatever may have been the
truth about their background, their imprisonment and execution made a terrific impact on life in the Red River
Valley.

For one thing, it gave a breathing spell to the bloody
feud enveloping Pilot Grove and the Corners. The people
were experiencing a revulsion from crime and fear of its
consequences. Neither Peacock, the scheming Union politi-
can hungry for power, nor Lee, the defeated cavalry captain
anxious to regain what was lost, made any public statement
about the hangings. The interlude attendant on the public
executions gave them time to plan their next move if they
chose to use it so.

On March 28, two days after the hangings, that move was
disclosed. A military posse rode out of Sherman to Mc-

57

Kinney, where they joined the sheriff and his deputies and a detail of citizens. The party rode north five miles to the home of Colonel William Fitzhugh, where it was thought two desperadoes, Bill Penn and Dow Witt, were hiding. The skirmish took place on a dark and stormy night. There were thirty men in the posse that left McKinney at ten p.m. under the leadership of Sheriff Wilson and Deputies Short and Hall, to a spot north of McKinney where they had been tipped off the outlaws might be found. One newspaper said the place was the home of the "Widow Lewis," and the other said it was the home of Mr. Beard. Both papers agreed it was a few miles north of McKinney. One paper says the posse stopped at Col. Fitzhugh's home first and made a search in case the ex-colonel of cavalry might be sheltering the desperadoes. Finding no one there, they rode north to the before-mentioned place. Surrounding the house, they demanded Witt's surrender, and that of Bill Penn, and their pal Hayes, first name never given.

"Suddenly and in a spirit of bravado and defiance," says *The Messenger*, "Dow Witt came out into the open prairie from the timber nearby, cursing and defying the sheriff and his party, discharged at them one barrel of his shotgun and then put spurs to his horse and dashed away.

"Ten or a dozen shots were fired in reply and a hot pursuit commenced. After a chase of four or five miles — in a heavy rainstorm — the fugitive was overtaken near a small creek which was swollen by recent rains. Dashing into the stream, Witt succeeded in crossing it, but before ascending the west bank, his horse was shot from under him and he himself repeatedly and severely wounded by Corporal Payne and Private Henry, who were foremost in the pursuit. Witt resisted to the last, emptying the other barrel of his shotgun, and one six-shooter, and discharging three shots (all that would fire) from another. He finally succeeded in sheltering himself behind a little knoll from the fire of the corporal and the private."

But the desperado's doom was sealed, for the sheriff and Sergeant McGraw had crossed the creek farther back and now attacked Witt from the rear and quickly "dispatched" the desperado. "So ended the career of another bad man."

The McKinney Enquirer reported Dow Witt "the desperado who has kept the people of Collin County in alarm for some time has at last been overtaken by violent death. He made a desperate resistance, using his weapons as long as he was able to do so, but at last was brought to the ground and killed."

In their pursuit of Witt the possemen had seen nothing of Penn or Hayes. They had started out to pursue the three, but one kept them busy throughout the stormy night, and it was not until the next morning that a smaller posse organized to hunt Penn and Hayes. Again, they rode out to the home of Colonel Fitzhugh. As they approached the house, Penn and Hayes ran out of the house and into the thicket nearby. Sheriff Wilson and his deputy, Wm. C. Hall, ordered instant pursuit, but they made the fatal error of dismounting from their horses and going into the thicket on foot.

Almost immediately, Deputy Hall and a soldier named James Johnson, were wounded. Hall was shot four times and severely wounded by Penn, who then took the six-shooter and Spencer rifle of the deputy, and with Hayes, his partner, made his way out of the thicket. The two quickly attached the sheriff's horse and that of his deputy and later in the day were seen trotting jauntily down the Rockwall Road. Of course the sheriff's party retaliated by taking the horses of Penn and Hayes — one of the horses was called a "pearl of the prairie" and was recognized as one that had been stolen from a gentleman at Marshall. Both the *Enquirer* and the *Messenger* printed full accounts of the raid.

MURDER AT THE CORNERS

One week later, on April 5, came news of the shooting at Alvarado of Ben Biggerstaff, or Bickerstaff, sometimes referred to as the "notorious desperado of East Texas" and "associate of the equally notorious Cullen Baker." Biggerstaff's home was in Titus County where his parents were highly respected pioneers of the county. Some six or eight months before, in the fall of '68, Biggerstaff and his companions had held up and robbed a commissary train that was en route from Austin to Sulphur Springs. The skirmish took place near Sulphur Springs, and in the melee that followed, Biggerstaff was almost captured by the Military. He fled to greener fields and safer highways.

The Military was unsuccessful in locating his hiding-place even though they thought they had him once or twice; their next move was to go into Titus County and arrest Ben's father. After keeping him in jail some time, they released him on bond that he was never to speak to his son Ben again.

When Ben was shot at Alvarado, *The Waxahachie Argus* stated: "Ex-Rebels and not U.S. Soldiers Do the Deed." The *Waco Register* got out an EXTRA edition to relate the "FEARFUL TRAGEDY," saying: "Biggerstaff came to Alvarado last fall and assumed the name of Thomason, but by January it leaked out that he was really Biggerstaff. People stood in terror of his name. Little was said of him openly or publicly. He never mingled with a crowd and rarely approached anyone unless he recognized some friend when he might come within a few paces, with his hands on his pistols and his eyes alert."

The Argus said that "The citizens of the village banded together, provided themselves with shooting apparatus, and on the evening of April 5th waited the arrival of Biggerstaff at his customary hour of sunset. When he arrived and hitched his horse at the hitching rack, he was met with a shower of bullets. As he fell prostrate and dying he gasped out: 'You have killed as brave a man as there is in the South.' " He made one final effort to fire his six-shooter, but his shot was wild.

The Register summed up the matter by saying: "He had elected to live a highwayman and had declared he would not be taken alive. He was thirty years of age, of slight build, weighing only about 135 pounds. He had a wife, said to be a handsome woman and reported to be living in Hill County."

Ben Biggerstaff was known by many people at the Corners and the news of his death had another sobering effect on the cringing populace. Then, too, in the middle of April, Deputy Sheriff Billy Hall of Collin County died of the wounds he had received in the skirmish with Penn and Hayes. Hall was a popular and respected man, and indignation against Penn, who had done the shooting, ran high. Coupled with it was the demand that the authorities, both Civil and Military, bring Penn and Hayes to justice without delay. The fact that the two were known to be members of Bob Lee's party served to increase the accusations against the man in Wildcat Thicket.

The agitation culminated in a handbill being posted on the courthouse doors in all four towns: Sherman, Greenville, Bonham and McKinney, reading: "ONE THOUSAND DOLLARS REWARD." It was dated Greenville, April 8, and offered one thousand dollars for any member of the Lee Gang delivered at Greenville Headquarters with satisfactory evidence that the captive was a member of Lee's party. The order was signed by Lemuel Pettee, Captain, 29th U.S. Infantry.

Penn and Hayes realized their days were numbered. Like the words of John Thompson's Dying Declaration, they knew their sins "had scented them out." They determined that nobody was going to collect one thousand dollars on either of them. Result: they took off for the brush country of the Red River bottoms, or the safety of the Indian Nation or Mexico. Nobody knew, but one sure fact was they dropped out of sight.

But not for long. In less than two weeks a fast-traveling rumor spread like a prairie fire through Grayson and Fannin counties: Penn and Hayes had been seen at a farmhouse in the woods near the river bottom north of Bonham. A posse was forming to go in search of them; it was to be made up of the sheriffs and deputies of the two counties, a group of citizen-volunteers and a detail of the Military.

On the night of April 20, the posse rode fast and north to the house where they had been told the desperadoes were hiding. The house in the woods was near the mouth of Bois d'Arc Creek in the northeastern corner of Fannin County. The men surrounded the house and called on Penn to come out and surrender, even though they were not certain he was inside. But their information had been right; the door opened and Penn came out. One man told that Penn was holding a lighted lamp in his hands, but this was not true. What Penn held in his hands were his trusted six-shooters. Penn spoke to the possemen as if he were expecting them. Perhaps it was a scheme for a quick bluff and get-away; nobody knew. Hayes was at Penn's heels with his pistols in hand, but he said nothing. The posse ordered Penn to throw up his hands, which he did immediately, but each hand held a six-shooter. He started advancing and firing at the same time. The attackers returned the fire, and Penn was hit. Immediately Hayes dropped his pistols and ran for his life. His quick eye had caught sight of one man in the encircling line who had no gun. Like a streak of fire he darted past this man and escaped into the darkness. Nobody followed; all were too concerned with Penn.

Men of the posse closed in on Penn; he was down and

several members of the party drew nearer to see if the noted outlaw of Grayson County was dead, or faking. Bill Everheart, who later became sheriff of Grayson, was one of these. He and Penn had been friends from childhood but were on opposite sides since the end of the war.

As Everheart bent over the prostrate form, Penn recognized him and with a feeble smile whispered: "You got me, Bill." Then suddenly with a last dying gasp, Penn fired a shot from his six-shooter. The bullet grazed Everheart's ear, and went through his hat; he was literally touched by death and Penn's last act was his attempt to kill an old friend.

The Bonham State News gave the headline *GONE UP!* to its report of the incident, saying that two men had met a party of ten men on their way to Sherman with the dead body of Bill Penn in a wagon. The paper gave further report that "Penn was said to have died game."

Penn's body was not taken to Sherman but to his mother's home in the village of Kentucky-town, where it was given secret burial at night in the old cemetery near the village. Bob Lee had lost a follower who at least was valuable for his marksmanship when needed. Very little was ever printed about Bill Penn, but his life story grew into a legend that is still known today in Grayson and Fannin counties. He was a dashing young fellow of good family who was killed at twenty-two, in this bloody era of 1869, when life was cheap.

CHAPTER 6

1869

Attack From Ambush

THE REWARD NOTICE GNAWED HUNGRILY AT
the cupidity of both citizens and soldiers; it tantalized bushwhackers, scalawags, and Red Legs, and was even purported
to be weakening the loyalties of some Lee followers. One
thousand dollars was a fortune in the lean and lawless year
of 1869. Little else was talked about or thought about at
any place.

There was no visible evidence of weakening by Lee
forces, and statements to that effect were regarded as mere
braggings of the Peacock party. The loyal Lees, on their
part, countered with the authentic rumor that Lee's men
would never surrender and that the Military would never

take Captain Bob. But in all truth it had to be admitted that it was becoming harder and harder to keep that pledge. Lee's party was on the defensive. The thousand dollar reward now applied not only to their leader, but to any of his followers as well. It was dangerous now to ride abroad in daytime. Women of the party had to be constantly on the alert to protect their men. Theirs were the ears that caught and carried messages to the men in hiding.

On May 6, *The Sherman Courier* reported that Officer Goode and his special posse had captured William Beard in the Indian Nation, and had got back to Sherman with the prisoner. Beard was reported by them as being a member of Bob Lee's party and was to be sent under heavy guard to Greenville, for possible claim of the reward money. Another newspaper of the area reported that Beard was being taken to McKinney. With that, William Beard vanished from the scene. There is no record that he ever reached either town; nor was any money claimed for his delivery to the Military. If he did belong to Lee's party, it is quite plausible to believe that members of the clan waylaid the guard, freed their prisoner, and went their own way.

It was just at this time, in early spring, that the flames of the feud flashed higher with a triple killing at the edge of the Lee land. Three Red Legs, fresh from Kansas, had drifted into Pilot Grove the day before, avid for a chance at the reward money. They had a conference with Peacock and other Unionists in the village. By means of the super-intelligence system of the Lee Clan, the news reached Wildcat Thicket within an hour. Road barriers were thrown up around the Thicket and the approaches to Lee land; all was done under cover of darkness.

When daylight came the scene appeared serene, yet the quiet of the countryside was oppressive. In the kitchen of Bob Lee's home, Dorinda Pierce and Melinda Lee were chatting about the day ahead at the Lee School. Dorinda was the teacher and was boarding at the Lee home. Her pony was saddled and waiting at the gate for her take-off, when the stillness was shattered by the sound of shots. Melinda wilted like a flower in the summer sun and whispered: "I'm afraid they've got Bob."

The young schoolteacher, according to the legend, answered with: "Why don't you go and see?"

The late T. U. Taylor in his articles in *The Frontier Times* in 1926, tells the story of these two "dauntless, intrepid women" who ventured out that morning to the Murder Road, otherwise the road leading from Pilot Grove to the Lee land. Their first glimpse of the road showed them also a man's body lying across the footpath. Melinda Lee, fearful of what she might see, stopped short, but Dorinda, usually called "Miss Dora," must have been a fearless soul, for she ran forward and knelt beside the body.

"He's stone-dead, Melinda," she called. "Come and see if you know him."

Hesitantly, Mrs. Lee came closer and looked down. She shook her head. "No, I do not know him," she said. "He is not one of Bob's men."

Without any more talk, the women went further down the road. They had heard more than one shot, and instinctively they looked further. Soon they saw another body, and then a third. All were strangers to them, and realizing that they were possibly neither Lee followers nor Peacock men, they concluded that the men were newcomers seeking the reward money. That being the case, they returned quickly to the house to give the report, but as no men had yet come in, they went back to the road and found nothing changed; no living thing in sight. They felt impelled to do something about the three dead men, so they stooped and pulled their hats over the men's faces. Even more than that, for since one of the men had been shot in the head and his face was a bloody mess Dorinda Pierce took off her white breakfast apron and wrapped it around the man's head. Then again they retraced their steps to the house where Dorinda mounted her pony and rode to the schoolhouse to tell her pupils there'd be "no school today." The teacher was unable to concentrate on the Three-R System at that time. She is said to have passed Bob Lee en route. Perhaps — and this is only hearsay — the riders paused for a momentary conference while "Miss Dora" gave a report to her chief about the three dead strangers she and Melinda had just attended.

At any rate, the bodies of the three Red Legs — for such they believed them to be — lay all day where they had fallen at daybreak. Peacock's men were afraid to come and get the bodies for burial; no Unionist would venture into enemy lines, and the ignorant newcomers had fallen at the edge of Wildcat Thicket. Certainly no Lee man would grant decent burial to a Red Leg.

So again, this time in the late afternoon, Miss Dora and Melinda set forth for the road; each carried a spade and hoe. As quickly as they could they dug a shallow grave in the ditch beside the road; then they dragged and rolled the three dead men into it, covered it with a little dirt and a great deal of brush and briers so that it would be indistinguishable to passers-by. Their task accomplished, the women returned to Melinda's home, and the three Red Legs sank to oblivion in a hidden grave.

The members of the Union League held a hurried meeting in Pilot Grove and, directed by their chief, Lewis Peacock, planned retaliation and revenge. They asked for, and obtained, more troops. Captain Charles Campbell and a detachment of the 6th United States Infantry were ordered to the trouble zone by General Reynolds. Their presence in the neighborhood added volume to the seething anxiety now prevalent in both parties, and focused more and more attention on the reward money. The Military had orders to settle the feuding in Northeast Texas by capturing the leader of the Southern sympathizers, and as many of his followers as possible. They expected the reward notice to be the chief means of accomplishing their mission.

Their strategy showed astuteness, and in some measure paid off. Lee's Loyalty Ring was to be broken, not by a Union Leaguer, nor by a bushwhacker, or Red Leg, but by a neighbor and erstwhile friend, Henry Boren, who lived a few miles south of Lee land toward Blue Ridge. Whether it was for avarice or personal hatred has never been satisfactorily explained. The Lees and the Borens had come to Texas together in the same immigrant train in the early 1830's and the families had been friendly, yet Henry was to betray the secret trails to Lee's Hide-out in Wildcat Thicket.

Came the fateful morning of May 24. Captain Bob had breakfast at his home that morning with Melinda, their five children, and of course, Miss Dora, the schoolteacher. It was a morning to entice one into the open country — dry underfoot, clear overhead and a gentle breeze blowing from the south; a perfect morning for a departure. It is entirely possible that Captain Bob had some secret plan known only to the closest members of his staff and family, for he came to breakfast dressed for the road. He wore his best clothes and boots, his black dress hat with plume and all his side-arms — his six-shooter, rifle, and shotgun. When breakfast was finished he announced that he was riding to a friendly neighbor's home not more than three miles away.

If his secret plan was to ride south to Mexico — and there join thousands of other Texans in exile — then he had waited too long to launch it. He had lingered on his rich farmlands of North Texas, pursuing his dream of independence and freedom until that road south had become

69

fraught with danger and death. Nevertheless, he may have been meaning to try it. Many thought so; family and followers would join him later in a country where they could start anew with their dreams of a horse ranch, a cattle ranch, and a cotton plantation.

It is told that Captain Lee was humming a song that morning when he came out from breakfast. Mounting his horse, he waved goodbye to Melinda watching wistfully from the porch. A happy smile touched Lee's features when thinking of his wife's love and loyalty; otherwise, his expression was solemn and sombre. This morning he felt he could sing; he felt secure, for his scouts had reported no skulkers in the Thicket, no traps in the brush where Unionists might have thought to take him. For four years they had been resorting to every means of trickery to capture him. Now he was riding out. Boldly he took the trail toward the road outside.

His journey was short. Less than half a mile from his home and before he reached the outside, he was caught by the flash of Federal musket fire from the guns of Captain Campbell's 6th Infantry. All the secret trails of the Thicket were covered by soldiers, and a few civilians, led there by Henry Boren, who is said even to have asked for the privilege of "first shot at Lee." Between eight and fifteen shots were fired and Lee slid from his saddle without a word. His horse was not hit, and at the sound of the guns turned and galloped back home, carrying the dreadful message of the empty saddle to Melinda. The shotgun was still swinging to the saddle horn. Melinda had heard the shots, and this time her worst fears were realized. "I know they've got Bob" kept ringing in her mind, as she went out to meet the riderless horse. Across the fields, Bob's sister, Minerva Lee Smith, also heard the shots. She turned and spoke to her husband, Martin, who was a preacher and a cobbler. "Martin," she said, "there goes brother."

The soldiers in the Thicket could hardly believe they had silenced at last the daring leader who had held the Unionists at bay so long. With muskets drawn, they advanced to the body which lay where it had fallen. In the heat of their passion they knew only one more thing they could do: take his effects and go. They took the gold coins and the gold watch from his pockets. Some clutched wildly to get their hands at last on some of the Lee gold which they had heard about so long; others took his six-shooters and rifle, and still others, his handsome boots. One unconfirmed story said the print of a boot heel was on Lee's face, put there by Henry Boren in his hatred.

Four hours later, by noon of the 24th, one of Bob Lee's brothers, and one of his young sons, were in Bonham and told the news to the editor of *The News*. The story appeared in the next edition of the paper, saying:

> This unfortunate man met with a violent death by the hands of Federal soldiers. A deadly feud, known as the Lee and Peacock war, was inaugurated in 1865 and has been bitterly and unceasingly waged since that time. The Peacock party was for a time protected by Federal bayonets, whereas Lee was outlawed by the Military, and a reward of one thousand dollars for his head offered by their commander. Lee then swore a vendetta against the Peacock party, and how well that oath has been kept, numbers of little hillocks, 3 by 6, in different parts of this and adjoining counties, can abundantly testify.
>
> We do not sanction, nor will we attempt to justify all of Lee's acts, but we would suggest that every honest-thinking person take the case home to himself and ask the question — 'What would I have done had I been so situated?' ere you give your verdict.

The McKinney Enquirer gave practically the same version of the killing as *The News; The Messenger* varied slightly, saying that the gold watch was returned to Mrs.

Lee and that Bob had no money on his person; however, nobody believed that part of the story, for the mystery of the Lee gold was known to everyone, and the public was determined to cherish its own version of the hidden fortune.

Parson Smith, Lee's brother-in-law, made the coffin for the fallen leader, and quietly and sorrowfully his relatives bore his body to its resting place in the Lee cemetery very near the spot where he had been attacked. All through the Red River Valley, the question: "What Will Happen Now?" was being asked by Southerners and Unionists alike.

The reward money was to go uncollected, for Lee had not been delivered to the Greenville headquarters, either dead or alive; the posse turned and left the body where it had fallen, taking only his six-shooters and his gold. The Military was to rule that Captain Campbell's men had done what they did while "in the line of duty." The archivist of the United States War Department stated in 1953 that the records do not show that any reward was ever paid to anyone for the capture of Bob Lee or any of his followers. However, the reward notice served its purpose in a cheap and flagrant way: it brought an end to the feud by appealing to men's greed in a desperate time when greed was common, and almost necessary.

Before Bob Lee was laid in his grave, there was a tragic aftermath to his death. An unconfirmed story, but one that was firmly believed by Lee's followers and others too, reported that the morning after Lee was shot, Bill Boren, a nephew of Henry Boren, rode up to his uncle's house at the usual killing-time — just after breakfast — and called to his uncle to come out. Henry made the fatal error of answering as requested, and was instantly killed by his nephew, who silently turned and rode away. "Death to a Traitor" was evidently the opinion of some of the Borens, and if Henry had hoped to enjoy his vengeance on Bob Lee, his joy was short-lived. Lee and Boren were both dead within the same twenty-four hours, and an apathetic nausea gripped the people of the Corners.

Without their leader, the Lee party ceased to function. Lee's former followers and trusted lieutenants scattered to parts unknown. Simp Dixon and Dick Johnson, son and stepson of Jack Dixon, could not be found. Lewis Peacock was said to be dreaming of a high political position for himself and had been heard to boast that soon he would have all of Grayson County under Republican control. It was just too peaceful at the Corners that summer to seem natural.

In September, a more normal tone came back into their symphony of life. A mysterious suicide occurred at a farmhouse ten miles north of McKinney, in the vicinity of the present town of Van Alstyne. It added a weird and grotesque angle to the bloody trail of the desperadoes of 1869. *The Dallas Herald* for September 25, relates the story under the title: "SUICIDE OF NOTED DESPERADO," although it cannot vouch for the name of the victim further than to state that "his name was either Hayes or Parker."

It was never proved which name was his, but there are many bits of evidence indicating that the dead man was Hayes, probably the same Hayes who had been in the gun battle near McKinney six months before, when Dow Witt had been killed, and Deputy Sheriff Hall had received mortal wounds. It was Hayes, the pal of Penn, who had escaped by running the gauntlet of the surrounding posse when Penn was killed in April. It is interesting to note the end of a desperado by his own hand.

On the night of September 10, two horsemen arrived at the Fields home about ten o'clock and asked for lodging overnight, as one of them was sick and could go no farther. The sick man said his name was Williams. His companion was a younger man of about twenty-two and gave no name.

Williams was so sick that he had to be lifted from his horse and carried into the house. He appeared to be about thirty years of age, slender, tall, short dark hair with whiskers — long upon his chin, short upon the sides, with long dark mustaches. He said he was suffering from acute rheumatism and it was obvious he had a high fever at the time. He was dressed in cassimere pants and a Yankee blouse. He said his mother lived in Morgan County, Missouri. The next morning he was no better, and his comrade rode off to get a doctor. He told the Fields he was going to the office of Drs. Shelburne and Dulaney and rode away toward Plano and Dallas.

He never returned, but he delivered his message to the doctors' office, and Dr. Dulaney arrived at the Fields home to treat the sick man. He left medicines and directions, and Mr. Fields was so concerned that he sat with the patient all Saturday night. giving him the medicine Dr. Dulaney had left.

The doctor came again on Sunday afternoon and found Williams much improved, with no fever and very little pain. The family invited the doctor to eat Sunday dinner with them, but the group had no sooner sat down to eat than they heard the crack of a pistol. They found Williams still on the bed with his pistol in his hand and blood flowing from a wound in his head. The family had left a small Negro boy to sit with him while they went to dinner. The boy said Williams asked him to hand him his saddle-pockets; he then quickly took out one of his pistols and shot himself in the head and died in twenty minutes without uttering a word.

A cap box was found in his saddle-bags with two lines scratched at right angles on the top. In one square was the name *Hayes,* and in the opposite square the name *Parker.*

In his saddle-pockets too they found some clothing, the two ivory-handled pistols, and fifty dollars in gold. Then of course there was his saddle, bridle, and a sorrel mare branded SH on both shoulders.

All this, of course, was good recompense to the Fields for their self-invited week-end guest. Nothing more was ever known about the sick man who, when he found he was getting better, took his pistol and ended his life. If he was the real Hayes, he knew that a thousand dollars was on *his* head too.

The editor of *The Herald* expressed his pleasure at the turn of circumstances in this unique comment: "One by one these outlaws are being removed, and we hope ere long to be freed of their presence," a sentiment echoed in rougher language by almost every resident in the four counties. The Lee and Peacock war was diminishing, vanishing, and yet there were to be several more bright flashes before the musketry cooled.

CHAPTER 7

1870

Dangerous Twilight

THE BLOODY, FRUSTRATED YEAR OF 1869 DREW
to a weary finish. Dismal and bleak was the gloom that settled over the Corners; its potent effects were felt in every
Confederate home. With Bob Lee gone, the Southerners
viewed their times with dismay. It was hard to realize that
the man who had been their leader and hero for four years
was no longer at the Hide-out in Wildcat Thicket to plan
and direct their efforts toward regaining their citizenship
and respectability.

On the other hand, the Radicals and Union Leaguers were
jubilant. Political control was in their hands and they felt
the magic of its power. Governor Pease had resigned in dis-

gust in September, and Texas had been governed by the Military for three months. The November election for the Governorship had been held for the few, under the strictest Military supervision. General Reynolds had magnanimously announced the winner to the people, but he had steadfastly refused to give out the figures on the election. Jack Hamilton had been counted out, and E. J. Davis, a strong radical, had been counted in. Hamilton supporters and a lot of non-voting Southerners firmly believed that Jack was the winner, but there was no recourse and no investigation. Confederate veterans were still disfranchised by the Iron-Clad Oath of Allegiance, and to them the November election had been a farce. E. J. Davis assumed the office of Provisional Governor on January 18.

In the Lee-Peacock country the Peacock people asserted their power in boastful talk and underhanded schemes of making life more miserable for Lee people. At the same time those followers of the gallant captain took some measure of satisfaction in the knowledge that no Union Leaguer, no Red Leg, Radical or carpetbagger had profited financially by Bob Lee's death. Nobody claimed the money that General Reynolds had advertised as waiting for some loyal man. Nevertheless, with Lee out of the way, the Unionist party moved into the open more boldly. There was resentment at their maneuverings and sometimes this resentment was voiced in other ways than gunfire.

For example, an unsigned letter to General Reynolds was printed in *The Dallas Herald;* its purpose was plainly to give the opinion of disfranchised Southerners. The letter could very well have been an editorial, but it was not printed as such.

Dear Sir,

As you are, practically, the Governor of this territory, or

satrapy, or State of Texas, we deem it right thus respectfully to address you. We feel, General, that it is alike in your power to protect or to oppress us as a people as your *will* — unrepublican as that may seem — is about the only law we have. These people (the Radicals and Union Leaguers) consider the state their oyster, and with your sword they desire to open it!

That desire for state control was the basis of contention between the Southern Democrats and the Unionist Republicans. The Radical party and its subsidiary, the Union League, drew their members from "the new citizenry," to-wit: Freedmen, bushwhackers, carpetbaggers, Red Legs, and Union sympathizers of all kinds, some newcomers and some long-time residents of the area. Murders and violence had increased alarmingly. The Military gave out the information that in six months of '69, murders had averaged one and one-half per day. It looked now as if 1870 might step up that rate.

There was some semi-official talk and many rumors that the Military would soon withdraw and leave Texas to the rule of Governor Davis and his Radicals. General Reynolds was reported to have had more than enough of the obstreperous country he had been sent to rule. The wishful thinking of the Southerners was that if they could get the General and his men out of the state, everything would be all right. The Corners of Northeast Texas, that had been so frequently referred to in newspaper dispatches as "the seat of war" now assumed a quiescent mood. Its grieving women nursed their sorrows and said little; its men carried their pistols and said less. Their quiet portended danger, for the "seat of war" was still a seat of war.

Miss Dorinda Pierce appeared to be the only happy person in the Corners. She spread her cheer far and wide. While men rode the hidden trails at midnight, she rode her little pony in the daylight hours to nearly every home within the radius of ten miles. Her business was teaching school, whether that was keeping the long term at Lee Station or holding a short session at her home in Pilot Grove. It took a lot of energy, ambition, and good humor to get up a school at a time when families were so torn by politics and war that education seemed a worthless bauble to them. But "Miss Dora" sold them her ideas of Reading, Writing, and the Rule of Three, with some history and literature added for the older pupils who wanted it. The number of students and the amount of money contributed determined the length of the school term. Dorinda had no trouble keeping busy, for her popularity and ability brought in the students.

Her closest friends and greatest interests were at Lee Station. She had lived in the home of Bob Lee and learned to love Melinda and the children. In the six months since Lee's death she had spent much more time than usual with the family. She was again, as heretofore, a source of strength to the young widow, and she made it her business to talk schooling to the children. She did her bit in lightening the shadows that hung about Lee Station.

Frequently she rode to Dixon's Mound. There were boys and girls there who needed to go to school but they were more needed to keep Jack Dixon's freight wagons moving and his twenty-four mules in prime condition. The Dixon family was one of those impoverished families struggling to meet the new conditions, and they had only Henry Moss and Jim Tate to help them. Jack Dixon himself had sustained a bad shoulder injury and could no longer make the body-shaking treks to Jefferson, and his oldest boy Simp was too well-known as a follower of Lee to take over the management of his father's freighting; the reward money offered by the Military applied to any member of Lee's party. Consequently, Simp was one of the midnight riders who dared not be seen on the public roads. People heard about his riding into various communities, but never was the story current until after Simp had disappeared.

Then there was Dick Johnson, Jack's stepson; he had ridden off to the West to look around awhile and had said he'd not return until life grew quieter at the Corners. He " 'lowed" he'd had enough fighting in the war and said he wanted a new chance.

Jim Tate was the Negro slave who had come to Texas with the Tate family in the 1850's. During the war he had come over to Mr. Jack's to "he'p" out, and the arrangement still held. Jim spent part of his time at the Tate farm, and part of it at Dixon's Mound. Jack and Sarah Anne were grateful. They had found they could trust Jim, not only with their wagons and teams, but with their little boys.

During the last year Jack had secured the services of Henry Moss, who acted as the straw boss of the freight line and the hired hand of the Dixon household. Already Henry and Jim and little Ennis Dixon, and sometimes even the youngest, Robert Lee, had made several successful trips between Christmas and Easter. Before each trip, Jack Dixon always checked carefully his merchandise for the east-bound trip — usually cotton, meat, flour and sundries. Just as carefully he wrote out his list for the return trip — lumber, dry goods, glass, and occasionally a valued piece of furniture, such as a piano or an organ or a mirror, shipped from New Orleans for some new home in the West. For every trip, Sarah Anne and the girls cooked enough food to last the trip.

The boys always took their little mongrel dog, Tippy, with them. Tippy many times played the part of a faithful messenger, for when the wagons reached Hog-Eye on the west-bound trips, Tippy usually disappeared. It was found that Tippy knew a short cut to Dixon's Mound, for when the boys and Jim and Henry reached home the next day after their usual last-night camp at Hog-Eye, Tippy was there to meet them. She usually reached the Mound at midnight, and scratching on the door as her signal, she informed the family that the boys were on their way home. The distance she traveled was at least twenty miles.

Miss Pierce, as friend and teacher of the Dixons, was cognizant of their business difficulties. Nearly every Friday afternoon she rode out to the Mound and often stayed overnight. Each time she brought books and exchanged them for books she had left on previous trips. The books were of various types of history, literature and arithmetic. She took time to give an arithmetic lesson to the boys, to re-read stories from literature with the girls, and, in general, to put the whole family in good spirits for the future. There would come a time, she assured them, when all of them could go to regular school, and in the meantime they must not neglect their studies completely.

It so happened that she was at the Mound on one of these periodic visits when the Dixon train headed by Henry, Jim, Ennis and little Bob, set out on one of its regular trips to Jefferson. The time was early February and the weather mild; Henry Moss had secured an extra hand for this trip and there was good-natured joshing going on while they readied him for the journey. She watched them ride away with a feeling of misgiving. There were so many dangers lurking on the high road to Jefferson. She wished that Simp and Dick could come home and help their family; the fact was that she was uttering a silent prayer that life in general would get a little better for the Southerners. It was nearly five years since the war had ended; the men were still disfranchised, and the state was still policed by military troops from the North.

Dorinda declined the invitation of the Dixons to stay longer at the Mound, saying she intended to ride that day to Kentucky-town to see about Miss Letha.

"Miss Letha," as she was known to everyone, was the sister of Bill Penn and lived in the village five miles to the north. In March, 1865, Letha Penn had married John W. Beven, a wandering soldier who had deserted her.

"Don't blame you, Dora," said Mrs. Dixon. "You might cheer her up. They say she still puts a lighted lamp in the window every night. Serves her right for giving her heart to that Yankee carpetbagger."

Dorinda saddled her pony and rode away; she recalled the story of Miss Letha and her lamp in the window, as she rode north to Kentucky-town. Nearly everybody in the Red River Valley had heard about Miss Letha and the trifling husband who had deserted her. Dorinda's heart was touched at the romance of it.

Nearly five years before, Mr. Beven had arrived in the community en route to somewhere. Some said he was a discharged Confederate from Missouri on his way home; some said he was a Union soldier from Kansas come to join Peacock's party, and still others said he was nothing but a deserter, a bushwhacker, a scalawag or a carpetbagger. But he had good looks and charm, and it was not difficult for him to win the heart of the sweet and docile Letha Penn, a popular, industrious girl who was highly regarded by everybody who knew her.

Of course, Letha was possessed of a few gold pieces which she had managed to save all through the vicissitudes of war; some thought her brother Bill had brought her the money from his forays outside the law. Letha also possessed a pony. This, and the gold pieces, might be called her only dowry. Within a month of their marriage, Mr. Beven took the gold pieces of his lovely Letha, mounted her pony and rode gaily away, telling his young wife he was just riding to Sherman to invest her money for her and that he'd be back about dark. Miss Letha set a lighted lamp in the window of their little cottage that night to guide him home, but he never came.

Five years and not a word from him, but she had never failed to light the lamp each evening at dusk.

Dorinda was enjoying the pathos of the story as she drew up to Miss Letha's gate. She hitched her pony and went in. She was hoping she could get Miss Letha to tell her love story because Dorinda herself was rapidly drifting into a love story of her own. There was a new schoolteacher in the neighborhood who was adding a lot of zest to her professional career. Jim Hancock had arrived from South Carolina a couple of years before. He had had a distinguished career in the Confederate Army with a South Carolina regiment, as had his father, who served on the staff of General Wade Hampton. Jim Hancock had left the old country for Texas and had spent a time in the West before arriving at the Corners. After meeting the popular Dorinda and talking with her about the future of Southern schools, he decided he had better settle here and help develop the school of the future. Wherever Dorinda got up a school, he got one nearby. They would consult and work out the new ideas together.

That had led to many social conferences, and Dorinda realized that such congeniality was bound to lead to something more than stimulating discussions of the late war, politics, and the need for more schools in Texas. Affairs of the heart now seemed paramount to her. That had been one reason she had wanted to come to see Miss Letha that day; here was one who had suffered the pangs of unrequited love. Its tragic outcome had not made her bitter or sour, or complaining.

Dorinda found Miss Letha busily engaged at her loom, which had been set up in the smokehouse. She, too, was one of the impoverished ones, and it was a case of nip and tuck to make ends meet. With her needle and loom and spinning wheel, she eked out her existence. As a seamstress she was in demand from the few who could hire their dresses made.

That day her mother, Mrs. Lindsey, was spending the day with her and helping at the loom. They gladly stopped work to entertain their visitor.

One thing was certain; there would be food to eat, for Miss Letha had home-cured meats, as well as potatoes, onions, peach preserves and biscuits. "And how're the folks at Dixon's Mound?" she asked after dinner.

"It's hard for them, Miss Letha. I feel sorry for those boys and girls. I do wish Simp and Dick could come home. Do you s'pose they ever will?"

There was a moment of silence before Letha answered quietly: "No, Dorinda, I'm afraid they never will. I'm afraid they'll go like Bill — shot down in some unknown spot."

In the early afternoon a storm came up, followed by rain and a norther. Miss Letha said it was too muddy and too threatening for Dorinda to ride back to Pilot Grove. She must spend the night. Mrs. Lindsey, too, although living much closer, gave up the idea of going to her own home, and the three women settled themselves before a comfortable, cozy fire in the front room. Dorinda was really glad about the rain; it would give her a chance to see Miss Letha set the lamp in the window. When dusk came, she followed and watched Letha light the lamps. She noted the extra lamp.

"Do you think he'll ever come, Miss Letha?"

"Yes, Dorinda, some day he'll come back. I'd hate to be unready. You see, if Mr. Beven should happen to come in at night I'd hate not to have a light in the window to welcome him."

"Oh, I'm sure he'd like that, Miss Letha. Do you think —"

"I think love is a wonderful thing when it comes to you, Dorinda," answered Miss Letha, taking the first lamp to the front room window. "Oh, but he had a way with him! And what a way he had with words!"

"Yes," answered the young schoolteacher. "I think I understand. I'm beginning to think I do."

There was no more talk of love and romance, nor of war and politics. When the three women sat down again at the fireplace, the talk was about quilt patterns and weaving; then there was corn to pop; and, of course, there were dreams to ponder.

Dorinda's thoughts were happy ones. Jim Hancock had a way with words too. She made up her mind that if he came bringing love she would not run away from it. "A wonderful thing," Miss Letha had said.

Letha's thoughts were sad and anxious; wondering when Mr. Beven would return, and keeping her ears tuned for the sound of a horseman at the gate.

The next day, when Dorinda returned to Pilot Grove, there was consternation in the village. The mail stage had come in bringing the weekly newspapers. She noted the little clusters of people at the stage stop, at the blacksmith's shop, at the grocery store. "Something's happened, for sure," she thought, as she hurried home. There she was greeted by her father, with the startling statement: "Simp Dixon's been killed!"

"Are you sure, Pa?"

"There it is, in the paper. Taken from *The Galveston News*. It says he was shot on February 5th."

"Where did it happen, Pa? And where's his body?"

"Somewhere out in Wise County, they say. As for his body, they don't know exactly. I just hope he got a decent burial. Jack can't go and get him. It's too far, and it's dangerous country out there. 'Sides, they don't know the exact spot."

"Was it the — Military this time?"

"No, daughter; the way they're telling it here is that Simp was shot by one of Peacork's men, a freedman, who trailed Simp out there and took him by surprise."

Shot down in an unknown spot, as Miss Letha had predicted only the day before! Another blow for the hapless Dixons, and another loss for the Lee party. Dorinda knew that there would be grieving at Dixon's Mound and at Lee Station for this man who had been so close to the Leader. She must make visits to both places soon. There was a possibility, though, that she might see Jim Hancock before that. He might drop by most any time. She hoped he would, for she had some words to say to him about neutrality. She felt it was his bounden duty to be careful of his words, in public, at least. She had seen too much of murder and vengeance and war to reach for more of it. Perhaps she had glimpsed a bright future that must be realized.

The news that Simp Dixon had been tracked down and shot by one of Peacock's men added fuel to the smouldering resentment against the Union League. Jack Dixon and his family said little; they neither admitted nor denied the reports, but just as Dorinda had surmised, they made no efforts to go and find the body. Time and distance were both against such investigation, but more than those, there was no certainty as to the spot where Simp had been murdered. The story of the murder was carried in practically every newspaper in the state under headlines of: "Another Desperado Disposed of!" and "Bob Lee's Chief Aid Shot Down on Frontier!"

The Dixon girls said they didn't believe a word of the story and that Simp would come back some day. Jim Tate said he " 'spected to see Mr. Simp come ridin' up mos' any time." Jack and Sarah Anne said nothing, but it was whispered around that they knew where Dick Johnson was, and if Simp didn't come in soon, they were going to write to Dick about it. Meanwhile, Jack kept all of them busy with his freighting.

General Reynolds was now actually what the newspapers had called him earlier — "the sole law within the territory"

— since Governor Pease had resigned in protest of the policy of the Military. The general, in January, issued a special order calling back the Radical Legislature in Special Session to complete the details of Texas' re-admission to the Union. This included the ratification of the 13th, 14th and 15th amendments to the United States Constitution, the election of senator to the United States Senate, and the lifting of the odious Iron-Clad Oath of Allegiance.

General Reynolds was in Waco when he received dispaches from Washington telling him the acts of his Legislature had been approved and the President had issued the proclamation. The General was so relieved that he handed the telegram to a citizen and exclaimed: "Here, take your State and run it." A moment later he added: "I feel like a great weight has been lifted from me. Thank God, I am through with the heaviest contract I ever undertook. I likewise wish the people of Texas the greatest prosperity." This story was first published in the *Waco Register* and reprinted in others papers of the state.

The citizenry received his news and farewell wishes with joy. There was friction and violence everywhere, but they wanted to solve their problems in their own way. It was not until April 16 that General Reynolds signed his own final order relinquishing all control over the civil affairs of Texas. Only then was it possible for a neighbor to greet another with "We're back in the U. S. A.!"

Nearly ten years of struggle were ending. There was a hope of peace. However, at Dixon's Mound there was little joy; Simp had not come back, and neither had Dick.

CHAPTER 8

1871

Final Flash

THE FOLKS AT PARSON GENTRY'S FARED BET-
ter than some of their neighbors, even though it was a larger
household than was customary or usual. What with three
sets of children — "his" children, "her" children, and
"their" children — there were twenty mouths to feed. But
there was always the Gentry farm to produce the food when
industry was applied.

The children were of all ages, ranging from John and
William, who had fought with the Confederates, to the
newest baby. Then there was Mary Anne Gentry Nance, the
young widow of Dow Nance, and their little boy, Johnny.
Blue-eyed Fannie was nine and the youngest of the parson's

first set of children; she was just six years older than little Johnny. All in all, it was a houseful of happy children, and life did not seem to be filled with the difficulties that beset their neighbors.

Perhaps that was due to the parson's strong religious convictions. He did not take sides on any question of local politics, but he did not hesitate to speak out on matters of religious faith and principles of Christian character. He believed that war was sinful, and in violation of God's law for man. His business was to work for the Lord, he said, and his ambition was to save sinners and change men's inner lives.

To accomplish this end he went about unafraid, and even unarmed, at a time when all other men and some women were carrying six-shooters. His preaching and strong personality had strong effects on all who heard him, whether that was from the pulpit, the front porch or the fireplace. He had come through nearly six years of war, local feuding, military rule, all mixed with much violence and bloodshed, and he was still liked and respected by both Northerners and Southerners, Unionists and Confederates. He rode horseback over a wide circuit which included Shady Grove, Pike, Desert, Pilot Grove, Kentucky-town and Porter's Church. He directed his preaching to Baptist churches already established, and in particular to the establishment of new churches wherever possible.

He wanted his children to have as good an education as he could afford to give them. Times being what they were, and his children numbering one dozen and a half, meant that schooling for the Gentry tribe was limited to the point of scantiness. Whenever he had any time at home, if not occupied with sermon preparation or field work, he called up his little group and instructed them in reading, writing and arithmetic. For the past year he had been one of Miss Dorinda's patrons, managing somehow to send Fannie and two of her brothers for a short term at Pilot Grove.

It was agreed by everyone that the parson was not only a great worker for the Lord, but also a practical man and full of common sense. He never lost his temper and he avoided politics like the plague.

His children were friendly with the Peacock children, the Tate children, and the Dixon children; in fact, there were no restrictions on who should or could not play at the Gentry place. Lee children came too, sometimes. All were welcome.

Emmaline Peacock, wife of the Union League leader, visited at the Gentry's now and then, but she was not a woman to indulge in social calls or chit-chat. Perhaps her husband's political career and his dangerous involvement in the feud with Lee had taught her to be always on her guard. However, she had been indiscreet enough to tell Elizabeth Gentry — the second Mrs. Gentry — that she was a Southerner by birth. She told no more than that, and in no way could Mrs. Gentry or any of the girls wheedle any further information out of her.

One day in late March, when spring was turning the dreary Corners into a bower of green beauty, Mrs. Peacock made one of her rare calls upon the Gentrys. She and John and Cathy were in the wagon and were returning from a trip to the store at Pilot Grove to get sugar and salt. As soon as the children were out of sight for a few minutes of play, Emmaline turned and asked Elizabeth and the older girls with her at the gate if she could leave some of her keepsakes and old clothes with them for a while. She would get them later on, she said, but right now she had no place to put them.

Mrs. Gentry and the girls agreed readily to look after them for her. They had space enough in the attic, they said, and it would be no trouble to anybody. Mrs. Peacock hastily took out some roughly-tied bundles and gave them to Mary Anne, who called up Fannie and told her to take Mrs. Peacock's things to the attic. The call was terminated, and Mrs. Peacock, John and Cathy drove on home.

The parson was not at home at the time of Mrs. Peacock's call, and when Elizabeth told him about it several days later he was shocked, displeased and sorely troubled, although he didn't say so.

He knew if it got out that he was hiding, or keeping, as some would call it, anything that belonged to the Peacocks, it would brand him as an ally of the Peacock party and an enemy of the Southerners. He pondered much about it and came to the silent decision that Mrs. Peacock's bundles must go back to their owner, quietly but as quickly as could be done.

Several weeks passed before he accomplished that purpose. In the interim he made several trips to the village, presumably to get some tools sharpened at the blacksmith's shop, or medicines at the drugstore, but more truly to listen to the comments of his neighbors. He became convinced that apparently Peacock's power in the community was weakening, just as the Radical party's power was declining in the state. Peacock had to do more talking now and with less effect than a year ago, and his threats and promises were likewise ineffective. Without the Military behind him he was diminishing in stature every day, even though he kept trying to bolster his followers with the empty maxims that he now had Grayson and Fannin counties in his hands and before long he'd have control of Collin and Hunt.

The parson was perturbed in spirit and he talked to the Lord about it while he prayed for peace at the Corners. He was thinking about that longed-for peace as he stood on his front porch one morning looking out across the fields. It was early June now and grain was ripening, fruit trees and flowers were in bloom, and there were indications of a bountiful harvest. Yet there was restlessness everywhere. Beneath this scene of quiet and beauty he knew that vengeance still was brewing. He kept asking himself the question — why had Emmaline Peacock hidden her belongings in his attic? Did she anticipate a quick get-away? Had she unwittingly betrayed some secret plan of her husband? If so, he must not allow his family to become involved. Turning back into the house he made his way to the kitchen where Elizabeth and the girls were engaged in the weekly baking of cakes and bread.

"Elizabeth," he called. "I think while you and the girls are finishing up your baking I'd better make a trip to town. Need to get some corn ground. And Mary Anne! While I'm hitching up the wagon you can bring me those things Mrs. Peacock left here. She's probably needing them and I can make it a point to go by and leave them."

He was glad that all the younger children were playing hide-and-go-seek, and the older ones were working in the fields, as he drove east toward the Peacock place. Elizabeth had placed a loaf of her new-baked bread in his hands as he mounted the wagon, saying, "Martin, Emmaline might need this too." Elizabeth had understood him; the bread would give him a better excuse for bringing back the bundles.

A short time later, when he drew up at the Peacock gate and called "Hello!" Emmaline came out quickly. "Good morning, Emmaline," said the parson. "Elizabeth wanted you to have a loaf of her new-baked bread, and I brought it by on my way to the mill." He handed her the bread and reached for the bundles in the back of the wagon. "And I brought back your things too that you'd left there. Thought you might be needing them." He hopped lightly out of the wagon and placed the bundles on the ground at the gate. "I think it's best, Emmaline, for more reasons than I need to mention, that you keep all your things together and on your own place."

"I understand, Parson," she answered quietly.

The parson got back in the wagon and drove south toward Pilot Grove. He was out of sight before the woman at the gate picked up the bundles and disappeared into the house.

In the village, excitement and talk were out of control. These stemmed from the rumor that Dick Johnson had come home and that Lewis Peacock was reported to have said that he was not afraid of any threat of Johnson's, and that "some morning when he goes out to get his wood for breakfast we'll get him." The parson found it hard to believe that Peacock had been so indiscreet as to boast of how he'd take Johnson. Also, he doubted that Dick Johnson had come back, although he did believe that Sarah Anne and the girls had corresponded with him. If either of these rumors had any truth in it, then vengeance was indeed brewing, as he had feared. He made it a point to wait and speak to Miss Pierce when she came into the grocery store. He cautiously inquired if she knew how the folks at Dixon's Mound were faring, but the young schoolteacher just as cautiously replied that he lived closer to the Mound than she did and besides, she had been right busy the past week.

"Tut, tut," the parson said to his mules, as he got into his wagon to go home, "these are bad times. I'm afraid my friends are moved by the spirit of the Devil." And then, from his habits and training, he uttered a prayer. "O Lord, direct these people to ways of peace. Let them forget the ways of war."

At home the children swarmed about the wagon to unhitch the mules and to peek into boxes and bags for storebought sweets or fruit. "Oh, Pa," cried Fannie above the din of the others. "Dick Johnson's come back. Yes, he has; I know he has because he rode right by here. I saw him and I remember him. Guess what'll happen now?"

"You children come into the house pretty soon," said their father. "And wash your hands. We're going to have special prayers before dinner. And Fannie, don't you be saying you can see a man riding by and know who it is."

"But I did, Pa," was little Fannie's final fling, not spoken until her father was out of hearing.

The parson made no further reference to the incident nor to the rumors he had heard in the village, but the children did think Pa's prayer was extra long that day; perhaps it was because they were extra hungry.

It was the next day that the parson saddled his horse, packed his Bible in his saddle-bags and set out for Porter's Church. Before he left he cautioned his wife, Elizabeth, and his daughter, Mary Anne Nance, to keep all the children close at home until his return. It might be best for all, he told them.

Meanwhile, as a matter of fact, precaution was being observed not only at the Gentry home, but also at other homes, as news of Dick Johnson's return spread rapidly to every part of the Corners. Some said Johnson had returned to kill Peacock, some said to help his folks, and others said to avenge Simp Dixon's death. Southerners said Mr. Peacock had better stop his bragging now, at least for a spell. Not many people had actually seen Johnson, for he kept out of sight in daytime, but a few had seen him in the yard at Dixon's Mound; a stranger was with him, they said. People stopped visiting, and few lingered at the stores.

The parson returned from his trip to Porter's Church and the next morning while he sat at the breakfast table with his family about him, the smouldering vengeance he had feared so long burst into flame. The sudden sound of shots split the air of that quiet June 14. Silence gripped the group at the breakfast table. The sound of shots was familiar to all but the very youngest. Fear held all of them in their seats. The parson forgot his composure to the extent of speaking aloud. "There, they've got Peacock, I figure."

It was only a few minutes later, although it seemed longer, that voices were heard outside. "Hullo! Hullo in there! Parson Gentry, you can go and dress the fowl! We've killed it!"

The parson quickly went to the front porch, but all he saw were three horsemen riding northward in the direction of Dixon's Mound. Slowly he turned and announced to Elizabeth that he must go to Peacock's place and corroborate the horsemen's greeting. No one else was to leave his house that day; orders that were eagerly followed by the members of his family.

The cry of "Peacock is killed! Lee's death is avenged!" penetrated every home of the Corners with mysterious speed. The details trickled in, bit by bit. Peacock had been shot to pieces when he went out to the woodpile in the back yard to get the stove wood for the breakfast fire. He was cut down by a fusillade of shots fired by three men who had been hidden in the trees of Peacock's yard all night waiting to catch him in the very trap he had described as suitable for Dick Johnson and any Lee follower. The men in the trees were Dick Johnson, seeking vengeance for the deaths of his step-brother, Simp Dixon, and his half-brother, Billy Dixon; the others were Joe Parker and an unknown man. All three were in hiding at Dixon's Mound. What was to be done about them, and what was to be done about the Peacock mess? Somebody would have to bury him, and then what about Emmaline, John and Cathy?

These questions were answered in peculiar ways. Of

course the parson would see that the shredded body of Lewis Peacock got buried. That was the parson's job; and the parson did what was expected of him. He did it in a quick but quiet way. Peacock's remains were buried in the old cemetery at Pilot Grove before the day of the 14th ended.

About Emmaline, John and Cathy: they themselves were not unpopular in the Corners but they were smart. The next day they vanished from the neighborhood, carrying only a few bundles of belongings in their hands. Perhaps the fine hand of the parson was involved in this plan. Nobody bothered to ask.

And the men at Dixon's Mound? Joe Parker and the unknown rode away in the night; Dick Johnson stayed on at the Mound. He conferred with Sarah Anne, his mother, and Jack Dixon, his stepfather, and his brothers and sisters. Neighbors, friends, and Lee followers made their way to the Mound and answered that question for him. They brought clothes, ammunition, and some money, and as one man they urged him to go North and stay until the clamor died down at the Corners. As a result, Dick Johnson took the road north and rode away to Missouri. He was not arrested nor even questioned by any officer of the law.

Flake's Bulletin for June 28 carried the following dispatch dated Pilot Grove, June 14.

Last evening a squad of men, three in number, arrived with double-barreled shotguns, revolvers, et cetera, rode leisurely into our burg. Their colloquial powers were limited. After staying a few minutes, they mounted their horses and rode off in an easterly direction. Since their departure, we are creditably informed that the famous Lewis Peacock, formerly chief-in-command of the Peacock Party, was shot to atoms this morning at sunrise in his yard. Political issues were not at all connected with this case.

You have heard of the foul murder of Billy Dixon at Hog-Eye three years ago, and also of the brutal killing of

Elijah Clark. These are the cardinal points that prompted the destruction of Lewis Peacock. May God grant this sinful world peace.

Since writing the above, it is all confirmed. He is literally torn to pieces.

The Bonham News, a strongly Southern paper, reported in its issue of June 16th:

"Lewis Peacock who is widely known in Texas as the former leader of a band of desperadoes and outlaws, was killed last Wednesday morning by a party of three men at his house in this county near the Grayson County line, two miles from Pilot Grove."

The Jefferson Jimplecute expressed the feelings of a great many people at the Corners when it said, in reporting a similar incident: "Our community breathes more freely being rid of these men that were a terror to all that knew them."

Thus vengeance, or justice, or both, was achieved, and the end had come in the seat of war that had vexed the state so long. An ironic fate had placed two great leaders as adversaries: Bob Lee, a soldier who wanted to be a peaceful farmer, was made a desperado by necessity, and Lewis Peacock, a politician who wanted to gain money and power, was branded a desperado by choice. In following these men, an unknown number had gone to their deaths — maybe fifty, maybe sixty, maybe one hundred.

In the summer of 1871, real and lasting peace suddenly came to the Corners. The Lees, Dixons, Gentrys, Pierces, Tates, and countless others, could face each other without fear or suspicion. The parson's prayers had been answered.

CHAPTER 9

1956

Repercussions

ECHOING THROUGH THE VALLEY FOR MORE than eighty years, the blasts of the Lee and Peacock War still reverberate and rebound from hill to hill and home to home; the prowess of the Lees, the loyalty of the Dixons, the power of the Peacocks, the faithfulness of the Pierces, the truthfulness of the Gentrys — all these appear again and again in the legends told by their descendants. Mostly, fears and hatreds have given way to pride and sympathy for the predicaments of their forbears.

There are many descendants of the Lees still living in the region of the Corners. Wildcat Thicket has been obliterated but nearby are the towns of Leonard, Trenton, and Pike, where you can easily find the Lee trail. Then also, there is Lee Street in Greenville to remind you of the early family that blazed its way through the thickets to found a settlement. Other Lee descendants may be found today in the cities, towns and settlements of North Texas. Some have located in distant states and metropolitan centers but wherever one is found he is likely to know the story of the illustrious Captain Bob Lee of Forrest's Cavalry and to take pride in recounting the deeds of the beleaguered after-war clan leader and feudist of North Texas. There are perhaps some personal keepsakes of the chieftain, such as a shirt, a vest, a watch, still in the possession of his descendants.

Few people ever knew where he was buried except that it was on Lee land. In the fall of 1952, the writer, in company with three other persons, Mr. and Mrs. Bruce Dixon, and Mrs. A. R. McMurry, who served as guides, visited this same lonely spot on the edge of Wildcat Thicket in search of the grave of Bob Lee. If there had ever been a marker placed to the memory of the gallant captain-desperado, it had long since disappeared. The place, known as the Lee Cemetery, because it was located on Lee land, was enclosed with barbed wire and covered with weeds, briers, and brush from one to three feet high. The guides knew the location of Bob Lee's grave, and knew also that his father, Daniel Lee, was buried beside him. The father's grave was found with an identifying marker confirming it, but beside it and just to the right of it there was only an open grave. Instead of another bramble-covered mound, there was a gaping hole about three or four feet deep in the spot Bob Lee was said to have been buried eighty-three years before. There was evidence of recent digging, for the ground was soft and no weeds were growing; not far away, a road map, a pamphlet about the U.S. Air Force, and some recently opened cans of pork and beans were found to bolster our suspicions that somebody had been digging for the Lee's gold, in the belief that it had been buried with the body of Bob Lee. The legend states that only three people knew the location of the buried treasure: Bob Lee, his father, and one of his sisters. When Daniel Lee was shot from his horse in a running gunfight on the Bonham road in 1877, the sister, already seriously ill at her home, died from shock upon hearing the news of her father's death. The secret of the buried gold died with her. To this date the Virginia gold of the Lee family has not been found.

As for the Peacocks, this writer has never found a trace of Emmaline, John or Cathy. Tradition says that on the morning Peacock was shot, Emmaline ran out to the woodpile and heard the words: "There's your old fowl; come and get it," from the invisible marksmen in the trees. Peacock was buried in the old Pilot Grove Cemetery, and Mal Jackson, who lives on the Binion place south of the village, can identify the spot; there is no marker, or other indication of a grave. The man who had longed for power and position sank into the quiet dust, and his wife and children stepped out into a protective oblivion.

And what of the happy Dorinda? She married her schoolteacher-confrere, Jim Hancock, on July 4, 1872. Parson Gentry officiated. The couple lived their entire married life in the vicinity of the Corners. They reared a large 'family of sons and daughters and their descendants are to be found throughout the area today. Some have followed the teaching profession like the studious Dorinda; others are numbered among farmers and merchants. One had a career as a United States naval officer. They take a just pride in tracing their lineage from John Hancock and Benjamin Pierce. To them, the parts played by Dorinda and her brother, the doctor, in the Reconstruction Period following the War Between the States are but illustrious incidents in their American heritage.

MURDER AT THE CORNERS

Jack Dixon, the freighter, lived only a few months longer than his arch-enemy, Lewis Peacock. Jack died peacefully at his home in November of 1871; Sarah Anne lived until 1899. Their graves are in an inaccessible, deserted cemetery east of Whitewright. There, too, is the grave of their son, Billy Dixon, a victim of the feud at sixteen.

Mal Jackson recalls that Dick Johnson returned from Missouri after a few years and settled on Dixon land near the old home at Dixon's Mound. He was a small fellow and never very talkative. He always carried his rifle, the same one he had used for Peacock — a single-barrelled cap and ball. It was a cumbersome weapon that must have weighed near twenty pounds, but it was never farther than reaching distance from Johnson. Jackson heard him tell the story of Peacock's murder.

There are Dixons living today in the vicinity of their forbears, and some very near the old Dixon's Mound. Most of them know about the connection of their family with the Great Feud but they are reluctant to tell it unless they are sure of sympathetic listeners.

Parson Gentry has many descendants living in the counties of Fannin, Collin and Grayson. A portion of the land homesteaded by him in 1844 is still in the possession of his descendants who are engaged in planting and harvesting wheat, cotton and corn from its acres, as has been done for so many years. The fertile land on Desert Creek is evergreen and bountiful.

Fannie Gentry Golden, the parson's daughter mentioned frequently in this book, lived to the age of ninety-two. When she died in 1954, she was lovingly called "Aunt Fannie" by her friends and neighbors in the Nobility Community, a few miles south of the Gentry land. She lived alone for many years in a small cottage next door to the Baptist Church. She was never afraid because the Lord was there, she said, and He was a pretty big Person and would not let any harm come to her. None ever did. She gave the land on which the church was built, following the principles of her father in establishing churches.

Time did not treat Letha Penn as kindly as it did Fannie Gentry. "Miss Letha" lived until 1914 in her little house in the village of Kentucky-town. For over forty years she kept the vigil with the lamp in the window, but her lighthearted, wandering husband never returned. Her life was lived in somewhat dire circumstances and in a constant struggle to make ends meet; yet her friends were legion and her memory is fresh. Today her name is spoken with affection by those who knew her and those who only heard about her. Her grave is in the old, deserted cemetery southeast of Kentucky-town, beside the unmarked grave of her brother, Bill Penn. Bill's part in the Lee-Peacock controversy was never mentioned by his contemporary relatives and is unknown to some of the family's descendants of today. Unlike his sister, his name is whispered carefully by people who have heard only bits of his tragic story.

Uncle Jim Tate, who was friendly to all parties in the feud and who came through the war unscathed, acquired a few acres of his own across the fields a couple of miles from the Tate land. He lived a happy life to the age of ninety-five. In the fall of 1952, when he was nearing ninety-three, he met Bill Stone again after a lapse of more than fifty years. Bill Stone, who was W. N. Stone to most people, was the same age as Jim, and the two began reminiscing of the friends they had known at Pilot Grove and Trenton. Uncle Jim gave his conclusion of the whole matter of the feud by saying: "There wasn't a finer gentleman anywhere than Bob Lee, but the folks just wouldn't let him alone; I don't know why; and Mr. Peacock — why I jus' loved him. He jus' got mixed up with the wrong sort of folks, I guess.

An' the Dixons — why, I worked for Mr. Jack and tended his mules and wagons. He was a fine man. I jus' don't know why people wouldn't leave him alone."

Mr. Stone, who had been a successful banker and merchant and had made and lost two fortunes, agreed that there was no explanation for the "great Pilot Grove difficulty" other than that it was the aftermath of the Great War Between the States.

Men from this region have been to four wars since then, but none has produced the terrific impact on community life as did the War of the '60's. Four years of declared war was climaxed by four years of deadly feud, initiated when Captain Robert J. Lee came riding home from Tennessee.

The echoes of that dreadful period grow fainter every year, and soon will blend with the harmony of the whole. The symphony of the U.S.A. grows stronger with the passing years.

THE END

Bibliography

Books

A Texas Reader, The Naylor Company.
Blackmon, F. W., *Kansas, A State History.*
County Courthouse, Bonham, Texas, *Records of Fannin County.*
Ramsdell, C. W., *Texas in Reconstruction.*
Ray, G. B., *Legends of the Red River Valley.*
Richardson, Rupert N., *Texas, The Lone Star State.*
Roberts, O. M., *Texas Confederate History.*
Thrall, H. S., *A Pictorial History of Texas.*

Periodicals

Frontier Times, May 1926 — March 1928; Texas History Center, University of Texas, Austin, Texas.
Index of Confederate Soldiers; Texas State Archives, Texas State Library, Austin, Texas.
Reconstruction Papers — Crimes: Fugitives From Justice, Anderson to Zapata counties: Murder and Assault With

MURDER AT THE CORNERS

Intent to Kill: 1867-1868 — Mss. Texas State Archives, Texas State Library, Austin, Texas.

State Land Office, Austin, Texas; Abstracts, Maps, Records of Grayson, Fannin, Collin and Hunt counties.

The Swamp Fox of the Sulphur, T. U. Taylor, Mim. Texas State Archives, Texas State Library, Austin, Texas.

The Texas Almanac, 1936; *The Dallas Morning News,* Dallas, Texas.

Newspapers

The Daily Austin Republican, Austin, Texas; Jan. — April, 1869; August — October, 1868. Texas State Archives, Texas State Library, Austin, Texas.

Dallas Herald, Dallas, Texas; March — April, 1867; May — September, 1868; April — September, 1869; January, 1870. Newspaper Collection, Main Library, University of Texas, Austin, Texas.

The Denton Monitor, Denton, Texas; August — October, 1868. Newspaper Collection, Main Library, University of Texas, Austin, Texas.

Flake's Daily Bulletin, Galveston, Texas; April, 1868; May, 1869; February — October, 1871. Texas State Archives, Texas State Library, Austin, Texas.

The Galveston Daily News, Galveston, Texas; May — December, 1868; April — October, 1869; February, 1870. Texas State Archives, Texas State Library, Austin, Texas.

The Harrison Flag, Marshall, Texas; April — June, 1869. Texas State Archives, Texas State Library, Austin, Texas.

The Standard, Clarksville, Texas; April — September, 1869. Newspaper Collection, Main Library, University of Texas, Austin Texas.

The Texas News, Bonham, Texas; January — July, 1869. Newspaper Collection, Main Library, University of Texas, Austin, Texas.

The Waco Register, Waco, Texas; April, 1870. Texas State Archives, Texas State Library, Austin, Texas.

Index

www.ingramcontent.com/pod-product-compliance
Lightning Source LLC
Chambersburg PA
CBHW071351090426
42738CB00012B/3084